SUNLIGHT
AND
SHADOWS

Essays and Stories on the Out-of-doors

SUNLIGHT AND SHADOWS

Essays and Stories on the Out-of-doors

by Gene Hill

Illustrated by Herb Strasser

Published by
Petersen Publishing Company
Los Angeles

FOR PETER ADKINS COMLY:
You have given me the ideal excuse to add to an ever growing collection of fishing tackle and shooting gear. I hope that you pass some of it on to your first grandson and that your generation will leave him a better place to enjoy it than mine has left to you.

ISBN: 0-8227-2965-2
Printed in the United States of America
Library of Congress Catalog Card Number: 90-61179
OTHER BOOKS BY GENE HILL
A Hunter's Fireside Book
Mostly Tailfeathers
Hill Country
A Gallery of Waterfowl and Upland Birds
Tears & Laughter
A Listening Walk
Shotgunners Notebook

FOR A GENERATION of sportsmen, Gene Hill has come as close to the embodiment of the ideal hunting companion as any man — someone as comfortable as a well-worn .410 who has the forgiveness of a bird dog and the patience of a priest.

His insights are often as much about life as they are about sporting endeavors. We see him — and we see ourselves — discovering life, puberty and the happiness of pursuit. He is one half humor and one half melancholy but always entertaining.

In "Alone," Hill reminds us how we began our passage through the sporting life and where we've come. "Going out alone was how it started with me, and that's how the circle is closing. I still enjoy hunting alone, accompanied by another overweight sportsperson who is living out this reincarnation as my Labrador retriever."

One look at Hill's soft eyes and it's not hard to imagine him spending his life as a Lab. In "Labrador Legends," we discover the humorous side of the author as he writes of his life with Labs. Through the written word, his Labs become our own dogs. "A normal-size Lab, about 70 to 80 pounds, will shed twice its weight in hair every year. . . .It is a known fact that if you keep a black Lab in an area where the primary colors are light, it will shed more; yellow Labs do the opposite."

Whether his subjects are dogs or deer, though, Hill reminds us of the value of time spent afield. Adventure — whether it occurs across the road or around the globe — is the very essence of the sporting spirit. It is in Hill's celebration of the smallest events in his life, however, at which most of us marvel — we do so because we understand that the value of our own experience does not have to be measured in distance traveled.

It is this reverence for simple, childhood adventure that we see in "Hunting Deer." He writes, "Like most of us, I'm not really hunting deer as much as pursuing a role, a pretend adventure that goes back to the boy I once was. . . .There are millions of us doing the same thing every season."

Perhaps the farther we travel from those roots the more we think of them. In "Special Spots," we find one reason why: "A common Indian belief held that every person needed a sacred spot, a place where one could be refreshed or made strong, or calmly think things out to a solution — a place where one felt happy and secure."

Here, in the pages of this book, is one such place.

November duck season in California. I remember it well. That wide open desert is a long way from my eastern waterfowling in more than one way.

○ *ALONE*

WHEN I WAS A BOY, I mostly hunted alone, in the company of the farm dog who tagged along partly for personal amusement and partly out of a sense of responsibility. Hunting then was a routine part of the day, an hour or an afternoon taken between chores. My gun might be found in a corner of the barn or in the kitchen by the woodbox, but always it was close by the other common tools—shovels, brooms, and axes.

Going out alone was how it started with me, and that's how the circle is closing. I still enjoy hunting alone, accompanied by another overweight sportsperson who is living out this reincarnation as my Labrador retriever. If you were to follow us, you could be forgiven for believing it an aimless exercise. You should see us plodding along a spring run for a while before veering off wildly to a patch of bittersweet or partridge berry. Later, you might catch us circling a thicket of popples or standing in the ancient randomness of apple trees that were once some optimist's idea of a farmhouse orchard.

What leads us here or there? To be honest, it's often whim or the chance of a downhill stretch in a cooling breeze; now and then, it's a sense of *something* that I flatter myself in calling *lore*. My experience has convinced me that I'm often as smart as a partridge or woodcock. My proof of this is that I can smell out a berry bush or a wormy wet spot, and I have taken pride in showing whitewash or scratching to a skeptical retriever who is usually more interested in urging me on to where the birds *are* instead of letting me brag about where they've been.

We find ourselves led here and there with as much art as a leaf blown by the wind. But we're alone and, most often, that's what we care about most. For all our apparent aimlessness, the dog and I know exactly what we're doing and why. Hunting alone lets us redefine things, outing by outing, hour by hour, or even minute by minute. Between the finding of the bird and the sound of the flush, I can decide to shoot or not; it all depends, and you know what it can depend on. If there have been only a few woodcock, you let the birds you find be, surprising yourself with the ease an unfired gun can swing through and make the perfect lead. If the grouse are plentiful and your thoughts dwell on a cold glass of wine and beach plum jelly on the side, then the nerves take over and the hands make little practice swings as the dog snuffles louder and louder the fox grape vines.

Hunting alone also means I didn't have to apologize for letting my dog behave the way I normally let her behave. I won't be embarrassed for shooting the way I normally shoot, or for sitting and just listening and thinking.

I certainly haven't forsaken the lovely days in the quail fields with old friends or the sharing of goose and duck blinds or dove stands, nor do I intend ever to give up the before-and-after arguments on shotguns as well as who knows how to use one and who doesn't, and why. I've never minded joining the laughter when I miss the easiest shot all day, or praising you beyond reality when you've been lucky enough to make the shot I just missed. And I'll always delight in seeing a partnership water over his hippers as he brings in decoys. But this isn't the kind of hunting I'm thinking about now.

I'm thinking about sitting on a deer stand and all the things that go through the mind when a yearling buck thinks it has outsmarted you—but hasn't. I'm thinking about a strutting tom turkey that spreads itself out like a rainbow and how the way the morning sun seems to set it on fire makes the decision for you. I'm thinking about the cock pheasant I can find almost any time I walk a certain ditch, or the covey of quail that I always stop and listen to on the way home, with my open gun over my arm and the lady tugging hard on her lead. I'm thinking about the knowledge of what is harvest and what is seed. These are the things best done when alone.

I've been hunting a long time, and I've come around to the idea that I really don't know much about most of it. I'm going out alone these days, to try and learn more. There are things I want to take home from the woods that I can't cook.

I'm beginning to learn something about dogs that I should have seen years ago. I'm beginning to learn what it's like to grow older,

and I think I'm beginning to understand that the great hunter doesn't really pursue as much as he lets things happen. He doesn't force events as much as he knows where and when they will take place. He is the wind and the stone; he is the hawk and the mouse. Hunting alone has taught me that where I want to go is so far I'll never find it.

After a day of hunting alone I like to spend some time with the soft hours of night when the wind lays down and I can look at the evening star. I like to stand there and think about my day, knowing as we all do that there might never be another one like it.

I remember an evening in the Colorado Rockies when I left the camp after supper to walk off the biscuits and gravy. I hadn't planned to enter the woods, but under the spell of a full moon I went back to stand near a beaver pond where I watched the silver reflections on the water. On the return to camp I saw something that made me stop. Not far from me a bull elk came out to graze, made free by the night and by a trust I clearly felt. We had a truce, a sort of magic of the night. We were here together but alone. I think we both found what we were looking for.

○ *HAIR OF THE DOG*

I'VE JUST read an article about a lady who does something really worthwhile with the hair from her faithful gun dog. Instead of pitching it in the stove or packing it in garbage bags, this enterprising lady has been weaving it into high-fashion jackets and even into nifty scarfs and caps. This gives that old saw about "the hair of the dog" an entirely new and wholesome meaning.

I don't know about you, but I wouldn't look any better in a whole coat of canine hair than I do in the handfuls of hair that decorate almost everything I wear. Maybe if I adopted the "his and hers" (or "his and his") look it might flatter old Gracie or Ned and make them steadier or less inclined to run deer. But then again, it might not. I am always a bit cautious about looking foolish in front of my dog.

The article says it takes about 2 pounds of dog hair to make a short coat. I assume that's about a size 8 or 10, not a size 46 stout, and I am sure I have to vacuum close to that amount of hair off my couch two or three times a week, not to mention the hair on car seats, rugs, and refrigerator coils, or the hairy tumbleweeds that drift across the kitchen linoleum, or pile up behind the doors and under the cabinets. I'm convinced there's enough dog hair in my house under the beds, in the cracks of the floorboards etc., to have raised the insulation factor two R's. I'd bet that if my house suffered a thorough cleaning (most unlikely), I could end up sporting a coat that would be the envy of a Russian czar.

The coat lady says she gets the hair by brushing, but I don't see any reason why you couldn't rig up something on your faithful companion like a lawn mower grass catcher, and just empty it every day or so. Anyway, I'm suddenly excited by dog hair. My dogs are doing something quite worthwhile; *they are shedding money!*

Being a bit of a worrier and a man who has spent a lot of time looking the proverbial gift horse in the mouth, I know that if I had a hand in this whole thing, something would go wrong. My hair coat would surely develop mange in the summer, or support a

thriving colony of fleas, or pick up burs from a considerable distance and mat under the arms. Worse, my friends would be sleepless thinking up bizarre remarks and hiding bones in my pockets.

The article says that a hair coat can be easily cleaned (unlike the original source) and if it gets wet, you just shake it dry (preferably, I suppose, on someone who has just put on freshly pressed clothes). Nowhere does the article mention anything about what a dog-hair coat smells like when it gets wet or whether it will float or sink when tossed in the pond (as I've had to do with my dogs after they have encountered the spoor of a horse or cow, or the ripe remains of virtually anything that exists in the hemisphere).

I wouldn't wash a hair coat while swimming, because every time I get involved in something I intend to be private, the UPS man or the fuel oil driver shows up, and there I am, thrashing across the pond wearing waders to test a theory, or hitting golf balls to a retriever so I can improve both our short games, or climbing up the kennel fence to salvage a fly that got hung up there on the back cast. Once, a delivery man showed up when I was playing the hose on myself to test a waterproof parka.

As far as I can determine, your wife can make cloth from dog hair by using her spinning wheel and then weaving the thread. I see no need for further investment there. If your dog doesn't shed fast enough (unlikely), the raw material is *always* there for the brushing. Most dogs I've owned would stand still and let you brush them until their ribs showed, although I once had an English pointer who was insensitive to being brushed with anything less than a heavy flushing whip. But pointer hair doesn't do much of a job covering even its original owner—mouse hair is mink by comparison.

The English setter has to rank first in sheer hair power, with the spaniels coming in a close second. I do wonder if a coat made of setter hair would be as adhesive as the stuff is fresh off the setter; if so, you might snuggle down on a sofa and have to be pried loose. I have not had any luck removing setter hair from anything but the setter. I used to keep an old suit that was plastered with orange and white hair against the eventuality that I might lose my senses enough to get another orange belton, but I put on so much weight since I quit chasing my own bird dogs that I can't wear it. I gave it to Goodwill and can only hope that an English setter owner who was both a 44 regular and needy—not an uncommon combination— has enjoyed it.

Looking for an excuse to get an English setter? The need for a dog-hair coat is as good as any. If your mind can handle it, two

Brittany spaniels would shed about the same.

No doubt this is an idea whose time has come. It'll take courage to be the first one at the gun club to sport a dog-hair coat, but there's always the satisfaction later on of knowing you were the first one to break the ground. If there's any problem, it's the possibility of your favorite gun dog giving one of his pals a nudge and a sly wink while rolling his eyes in your direction and whispering: "I gave that guy the coat off my back."

○ *COMMON INTERESTS*

A FRIEND RECENTLY sent me this notice from a West Coast newspaper classified section, and I think it deserves consideration as a somewhat mysterious voice from the wilderness that has both a pleading charm and a modern, let's-put-it-all-up-front-and-get-on-with-it approach. I'm intrigued with this notice on both counts:

COMMON INTERESTS
Fishing (love to fish for trout, etc.)
Would like to learn deep sea fishing!
White, blonde, 5'10" female, 45,
interested in meeting man with same interests. Also love
music of all kinds. Times Box G-25 . . .

Obviously this is a nice lady who is yearning for a lifetime of serious discussions on delightful topics like using the Adams as a searching fly, and why they don't make plugs like the old Pikie Minnow anymore, and if you only had one Dardevle to use, would it be the plain copper finish or the classic red-and-white? This is a lady who would like to troll through life listening to a little Mozart and perhaps Lefty Frizell or old Tom T. Hall. Who can argue with that?

When I was much younger, the lonely young men who wanted companionship went to a bar or a bowling alley. We should have spent more time hanging around in the tackle shop or at the dock.

Think of all the problems this nice lady would solve! You know what to get her for birthday and Christmas present; a new pair of waders would be appropriate every third Valentine's day. I can just see her opening a long, thin package by the tree, there's a tiny tear in the corner of her eye as she tries to guess if it is the 5-weight trout rod she's been wanting, or the new light casting rod for half-ounce jigs.

If I'm correct in reading between the lines, this nice lady has tried chatting up some of the West Coast trout and steelheaders—with little success. I can understand that, judging from the few I know. I don't think she would have fared much better in the East, either. I was fishing a fairly famous stretch of Eastern trout water a few years ago and the local gurus wouldn't even talk to me at first because I was using a fiberglass rod. They only relented when they found out that my rod was custom made by one of their gurus.

I can sympathize with an attractive woman and the equipment she wants noticed, whether or not she is wearing waders. "Hi there, I see you're using one of the old classic Hardy Perfects" would not rank with the all-time great introductions, but then a lady who has cast (!) her lot among trout fishers must realize that fishermen are rarely famous for wit or humor.

I suppose one of the reasons trout fishermen are so dour is that they rarely catch anything. Another is that the whole charade is about as expensive as outfitting a knight for the Crusades. Trout fishermen are too overly committed to have a rollicking good time. They've probably been reading Haig-Brown, Hills, and Skues, who are often thoughtful and provocative, but whose writings rarely make us laugh out loud.

Dare I even suggest that our fair lady might very well be a better fisherman than the merry band she finds streamside? If so, she would do well to conceal her skills for the time being; I have seen too many old friendships stretched and broken over such nitwittery as who can make the longest cast, or who has the most, largest, prettiest, etc.

My heart goes out to this blonde treasure, all 5'10" of her. I hope she finds a mate who will read to her of an evening from Kip Farrington or George Reiger, if she wishes to race the blood, or from Lee Wulff, or Phair or Leonard M. Wright, Jr., if she seeks meditation or inner calm. I can see her tying flies, wrapping a new boron rod in his favorite color, or happily patching a wader or mending a hook hole in the back of a fishing vest.

I suspect she also knows why she seeks a soul mate to take her

bluewater fishing. For a lady it might be perfect—the wardrobe expansion, the variety of fishing, the chance for better bathroom facilities, and so forth. And there is always the possibility that the average male deep-water fisherman is a more outgoing, athletic type than the river and stream laborer; the poet seems more comfortable with a 20-inch trout and size 16 elk hair caddis than a 9/0 reel and a pound of plastic squid.

We have to admire and respect this blonde lady. I don't know any men who are adventurous enough to run an ad like this. On the other hand, I don't know any man who wouldn't be considerably cheered by the likelihood of meeting a blonde, 5'10" female who is really interested in fishing, although they might be too awkward or shy, or too dumb to let her know it. Something is inherently wrong with the system; there are probably several million male

deep sea fishermen, yet a pretty blonde lady has to advertise her interest in meeting just one. But I have a good feeling that she knows exactly what she's doing. Most blonde, 5'10" females do.

If I were a betting man, I'd say that this blonde lady is already learning everything she wants to know about deep sea fishing, and loves it! I hope her "man with same interests" realizes how lucky he is that she had the gumption to roust him out of some tackle shop or boatyard where he was boring his buddies with old yarns.

The next time I'm in California near the town whose newspaper published the blonde lady's classified ad, I'm going down to the local fishing boat dock. I'm going to look for a boat with a name that's kind of a code, something along the line of "Times Box G-25 . . . " And I'll look for a blonde, 5'10" female, 45; she'll be with a handsome man who has the "same interests."

I may not see her—but I'll know she's there somewhere; she who "would like to learn deep sea fishing . . . Also love music of all kinds . . . "

One of my favorite guns—a 28-gauge hammer gun of no particular value except that when I use it doves fall—not every time, but often enough, often enough!

○ DOVE MAGIC

THE MEMORIES seem to get sweeter as the shadows lengthen in the cooling of the late afternoon. It's a time to reflect on each other's questionable shooting and to pick and pluck another dove from the small pile of birds next to the large pile of 20-gauge empties. The aging retriever, unable to take another step, is stretched out luxuriously in the shade listening to the stories and smiling at the best of the oldies.

At the family barbecue that night, it's plainly evident that the kids now consider themselves dove shooters; in fact, they are already becoming instant "experts." You can see yourself a few years back when you just *knew* you had a lock on those high incomers and you weren't too reluctant to tell others just how you did it. The memory brings a smile.

Dove shooters are about half convinced that those little birds were created just to bedevil the shotgunners. I'm typical. I *know* how to shoot doves; it's just that sometimes I *can* and sometimes I *can't*. That's part of the magic of dove shooting.

The ideal dove gun would throw a perfect 36-inch pattern of 8's at all ranges from 20 to 45 yards and wouldn't have any recoil. In other words, there ain't any such animal. If there were, the ideal dove would somehow manage to fly about 40 inches from where you thought it was, at a distance of 46 yards.

The beginning dove hunter will start out with whatever's at hand. Since he's a beginner, he won't do as well as he thinks he should, and since he's a typical shooter, he'll blame his equipment. If he's shooting a modified or full choke, he'll change to one more open; or vice versa. If he had a long run of three or four with 7½'s, he'll swear he's found the secret, until he runs through a box of those and ends up with five of six birds. Then he'll switch to 8's or 9's, or maybe even 6's—*anything* but those cursed 7½'s!

He will go camo from head to toe, not forgetting his beverage holder or the package his chewing tobacco comes in. He may even go so far as to tape the barrel of his shotgun and try to make his dog wear a little camo blanket. Most dogs, having too much good sense, won't wear one. He will buy and immediately lose a dove call. He will try decoys and then decide they're too much trouble. In short, he will do anything except work on his wingshooting. But this will not deter him from giving advice to anyone who is foolish enough to ask for it, or even stand still long enough to have him demonstrate the smoothness of his swing on a left to right crosser.

The problem for wingshooters is that the dove is the perfect, number 10, quintessential, never-to-be-improved-on target.

The average flight speed of the dove is about 35 miles an hour, and since these birds rarely just glide around, the reason you don't have enough doves for a second helping is that you're shooting behind them. But then you no doubt figured that out all by yourself long ago. Can I help you? Sure: get out in front more before you pull the trigger. And that's almost all you have to know about improving your average. Almost.

I am living proof that there are more ways to miss a dove than

any other gamebird, and I have personal embellishments on most of those. If you're experienced, you ought to know at least four ways to miss an easy incomer, and the same applies to a simple crossing bird. You can do better than that on doves coming overhead from behind you. All of these situations are subject to additional errors depending, in direct proportion, on how many other shooters are watching you and how you *discussed* your ability with a shotgun the night before.

A real, bedrock dove shooter ought to be nearly impervious to scorn and ridicule, and a virtual genius at excuses—not that anyone is going to accept any of them. If you haven't been dove hunting much, I promise you that the talk is *never* about how well you shot. If you have really done yourself proud, the chances are strong that you will be ignored for most of the evening, and rightfully so.

Ed Zern has always had problems compensating for the rotation of the earth, and never shoots as well as he should expect when he's on the Equator. Most of us who know Ed well accept this as a fact, and I'm not sure that it can be considered an excuse. Bob Brister (who really is a fine shot) will show up wearing a neck brace. If he shoots well, he can take it off; if not, we all sympathize and remember how superb he was before the affliction.

I am not unwilling to talk about how bad my back is *before* a dove shoot, and I will often start out shooting while sitting on a little stool until I discover which way my shooting is headed (my skills with a shotgun are akin to an opera singer's ability to nurse a high C). If I'm destined to have a fair day (better than 50/50 average), I'll stand up and announce a recovery; if not, I might mutter about how stupid it was of me to forget my cane.

In general, the intelligent dove shooter always has an excuse. No matter how well he does, he ought to have done better. *He never admits to shooting up to his average!*

An outside observer might be led to believe that dove shooting is a sentence passed down by a judge. At the end of the day, everyone is grumbling. The dogs are bleary-eyed and trying to learn how to spit to get rid of pesky breast feathers. Shooters make pronouncements about their guns being inadequate at best, and downright treacherous at worst. Even a man of the cloth might feign deafness if asked his average birds-to-shells ratio.

But before long the atmosphere changes. The picking crew is telling jokes and some of the dogs are arguing about who belongs under what pickup truck.

The talk turns to the mystical "next time," when the gun that was left at home will make all the difference, and when the proper leads, finally figured out in the softness of the twilight, will be pressed into use.

Dove shoots give us the special sense of brotherhood that comes with the gathering of the clan. There are other campfires we remember, but none are more significant, and few as sweet.

○ THE TIME
OF DISCOVERY

EVERY SO OFTEN, when I see an old Model A Ford on the road, I am instantly flooded with waves of unmeasurable happiness. I am back at the wheel of my Model A again, heading for my favorite woodcock cover, or inching along a snow-covered dirt road looking to see where the deer have been crossing, or showing off for the girls a little by shifting with my knee.

I know that dwelling on what's too long gone doesn't make a lot of sense, but then I don't see a lot of harm in it. Nostalgia is a little like whiskey; if it's taken sparingly and for medicinal purposes, it can be good for the soul.

I don't remember exactly when my father bought our Model A, but I do know it was secondhand, had been driven only a couple of hundred miles, and it was to be used as our hunting car. In those days you wouldn't have wanted anything better. The Model A was boxy. It was designed for utility and comfort, and whatever you thought of its looks was of no matter to Mr. Ford. You liked it or you didn't; America loved it.

The roof was high enough for a man to wear a fedora, and running boards were wide enough for a lady to enter and exit with modest grace. It had no heater or radio, only the essential instruments—a gas gauge, which was really a visible float, and a water temperature gauge, which was a sensible thermometer fitted as part of the radiator cap. The very simplicity of the Model A, its looks and lack of artificial pretension, lent it an air of and a reputation for great reliability, which it fully deserved. The Model A could do what it looked like it could do!

I started driving ours when I was twelve. I drove illegally, but in those days practicality and common sense were higher cards. I think that every boy I knew started driving when their legs were long enough to reach the pedals.

Our winter gear was an ax, for fallen trees across the road, a shovel, and set of chains. The chains were a nightmare. Not only were they a pain to put on under the best of circumstances, but like all boys, I generally put the job off until I was stuck somewhere, usually at dark. With my car there was an additional problem—the rear tires were of a slightly different size, and if one chain went on too neatly, then the other wouldn't go on at all, by half an inch. The chains were always breaking, and at the second of heavy clanking against the rear fender you had to stop and make repairs, always when the temperature was about zero, it seemed, and frequently when you couldn't find your gloves.

The ax and shovel pretty much stayed in the car year around, since they were often needed when I got stuck somewhere I shouldn't have been or tried to use the old car as a tractor. With a Model A you could generally get yourself out of trouble single-handedly. Maybe you had to cut a little brush for traction in the mud or dig a little if you got yourself high sided, but the Model A could almost drive itself while you pushed, since it had a hand throttle. The system was to set the gas as low as you dared, put it in low gear, let out the clutch, and then jump out, push, and jump back in again. I'm glad my mother never saw me doing this, although I don't remember ever denting a fender in all the years that the Model A and I ran around together.

And what places we went! I don't have any idea how many miles I drove over the more than ten years we had the old car, scouting for bird covers, looking for drumming logs, wood duck potholes, new bass ponds—just exploring in general, seeing how things were getting on. It's hard to explain just what a car meant in those days, but it was more than transport; it was finally the freedom to see and do some of the things that were always in one's mind. The Model A brought a reality to a lot of boyhood dreams.

If I have somehow given the impression that I could climb aboard whenever I pleased, let me quickly assure you that nothing could be further from the truth. I almost never took the car without permission and permission was almost never granted unless the chores were done, an almost impossible set of circumstances given my tendency to avoid hard work or at least postpone it as long as I could. But somehow the work got done and, while I've forgotten

what many of those chores were, I still remember the long summer hours on the lake, the woodcock covers, the rabbit hunts and the ancient excitement that can only be stirred by a trapline. Our old Model A was enough of an anachronism even when I was in high school to lure a girl now and then to go off on a coon hunt. I can still hear them giggling and squealing when one of the Redbones or Blueticks slobbered all over them, no doubt as intoxicated by the power of five-and-ten-cent perfume as I was.

The Model A wasn't the quietest running car, and in keeping with our country ways, it helped to minimize casual chitchat. It had, however, a comforting noisiness, a sound of honest industry under the hood that mirrored the mood of the time—work hard and you'll get to wherever it is you want to go. And in its own odd way, there was something undeniably cheerful about the Model A, in spite of its judicial black color and rather no-nonsense appearance. I think the cheerfulness represented the beginning of America's "good times" era—an atmosphere of "we're in this together" that was contagious. I suspect that was one of the reasons the girls liked it so much; its rambunctious air shadowed the time and the people it was really built for—flappers and their sleek-haired beaux carrying hip flasks.

We kept our Model A for almost fifteen years and sold it for about twice what we bought it for. The interior had held a few dogs too many, and the remnant smells of uncountable muskrats, coons, and fish gave the tattered upholstery character. The truth of it was that I was in college and my father had lost some of the passion for going afield when I wasn't there to be bossed and taught how things ought to be done.

At the moment I'm driving the closest thing in my heart to the Model A—an ancient van whose insides resemble a rather poorly managed hardware store. It should have gone to the junkyard a couple of years ago, but the fact that no one else in my family will drive this hulk any more makes it especially endearing. Anyway, we still get alone fine: neither one of us is in much of a hurry.

I know that if someone were to offer me a Model A today, I'd have to say, "No, thank you." Because I don't really miss the Model A; I miss the time of discovery that came with it, the sense that there really weren't any places I couldn't go to hunt and fish and look around—after the chores were finished.

○ *THE GIFT*

I HOPE MOST OF YOU can remember a Christmas made special because a certain longing was satisfied in an unforgettable way—something more than a present, more than a surprise.

I've always been partial to stories about kids seeing odd-shaped packages under the tree and knowing, just *knowing* that Grandpa or Dad had finally come through with the old 20 gauge or a fly rod or a puppy, usually unwrapped. At the moment, I don't remember ever seeing any such parcel under the tree with my name on it. I do recall getting a Flexible Flyer which was very much wanted but not all that much of a surprise. I don't recall any kid of that era being truly surprised by a Christmas package. The barns and various sheds and the house were under such strict surveillance that if a new field mouse moved in we knew about it, much less a bicycle or a fly rod or a shotgun.

Back in Depression times when the average American factory worker earned less than $1,000 a year, and the average farmer less than that, presents for small boys tended to fall into the "What does he need?" category. Luckily, "need" could sometimes stretch to cover No. 1 Blake & Lamb traps, a pocket knife, or new rubber boots; it might even stretch as far as an adventure book about Africa or the Far North or the mysterious ocean, if you had any reputation as a "reader."

Our Christmas Days seemed noisier then. The kitchen was overstuffed with ladies cooking too much food. The men argued about horses and guns and dogs, and the kids wrestled around underfoot until they were shooed outside to do chores or play games. The farm dog had been waiting for them on the porch since dawn.

The normal procedure in our house was that no present could be fooled with until Christmas morning. No jiggling of any boxes under the tree (we did, of course). We were given one present to open after supper on Christmas Eve—just one and no second guessing. We usually had a rough idea of what was in the box; at worst it wasn't more risky than picking out a piece of chocolate and hoping it wasn't filled with jelly. What we didn't want to get stuck with was a piece of clothing. Chances were it would be handmade and we would have to try it on. The workmanship would be praised.

And we would act surprised, in spite of the fact that we were frequently measured all summer and fall by the local seamstresses and knitters, who hoped their guesses on rate of growth had been correct and that the garment could be let out, if it lasted long enough.

When it was my turn on this particular long-ago Christmas Eve, I pointed to a box that had just arrived with a favorite aunt who seemed to be especially fond of me. The fact that she rarely saw me may have influenced this relationship. She was capable of real surprises. Once, against my family's advice, she gave me a BB gun. Another time she gave me a doughboy's helmet from World War I. I knew which package was from her and I was about to open it when my father took it away and handed me another one. "I think you'll like this one," he said. In a box far too large to afford the smallest clue, wrapped in several old copies of *Fur, Fish & Game*, was my much-wanted flashlight!

A flashlight may not seem very exciting unless you grew up in a house that was lit by kerosene lanterns, with toilet facilities located a considerable distance away from the house. The flashlight allowed you to read in bed when you were supposed to be asleep gathering your strength for chores. And, you could put the lighted end in your mouth, sneak into your little brother's room late at night, and scare him witless! Somehow, having a flashlight changed your life a little in those days. Kids who had flashlights were no longer supposed to be afraid of the dark; you were growing up, however slowly.

Before I got my flashlight, my father wouldn't take me coon hunting. Of course, I was too small to keep up with the men. It must have hurt my father to keep saying *no* when it was obvious that to be permitted to tag along was one of the things I wanted most in the world to do. On the nights when the men hunted, I would lie awake with my head on the sill of the open window, straining to hear old Red barking, but I never did.

"You're not big enough to have a flashlight," my father would tell me. It must have seemed a softer thing to say to a boy than to remind him endlessly that he was too big to carry and too little to go it alone. But that was over now. I was finally big enough. My father's excuse no longer worked.

I ran out of the house without remembering to say "Thank you," and stood on the lawn shining the topmost branches of the maple tree. Red, no doubt excited by the light, let out long rolling moans from his kennel run. My father came out and we agreed that the flashlight was perfect—perhaps the best one he'd ever seen. Red started a low chopping bark. "He thinks we've taken over his job," Pop said. Then, after a minute or two of silence, he said: "Why don't you go get your boots and coat and put Red in the car?"

I knew the field like the back of my hand from fetching water to the haying crew, but the mystery of the strange shadows cast by the full moon through the fingers of the drifting fog was compelling. We stood there listening to the ghost voices of owls while Red sorted through pungent footsteps of possums and skunks. We waited in silence, wondering if I was really big enough to be coon hunting, and if so, should I no longer hold my father's hand.

My father swung me up on his back when Red started barking treed. I clung like a monkey with one hand, holding my flashlight ready with the other in case my father needed to see where he was going. Red quieted down when we reached the tree and Pop and I both shined our lights from branch to branch. My light found one golden dot and then another. The coon was peering down from a dark hollow near the top. My father told me to stay where I was and then he left. If I had any thoughts about being left there alone with Red, I kept them to myself. I didn't ask where he was going, either. Men don't bother each other with trivial questions.

My father came back carrying a ladder he'd borrowed from a nearby farm. He leaned the ladder against the tree, climbed up, peered into the hole, and then called down for me to join him. When I reached the top of the ladder, he held me up so I could shine my light into the hollow. There were two pairs of eyes. "It's a mother and her baby," I said. And that's all I dared say, knowing full well that a good part of our income came from my father's trapping and coon hunting. But he knew what I had said. I turned off my flashlight, put it in my pocket and waited until my father reached the ground and threw a light on the ladder so I could see, my short legs fumbling for the rungs. On the ground my father knelt and I swung my legs around his neck. He picked up the ladder with one hand and walked back to the Model A. My flashlight lit the way. While I waited for Pop to return the ladder, I showed Red my flashlight and promised him that this was just the first of many hunts. Red fell asleep, but I kept my light on, just in case.

When Pop came back, I climbed up on his lap and worked the choke on the Model A for him. We drove home, my hands under his on the steering wheel.

Memories accumulate under the weight of added Christmas Eves. But every time that night comes, I go off by myself for a while and remember the smell of the night air and the echo of Red's voice in the dark. I look at the tree brooding over the ribboned boxes and remember with a terrible yearning that I was fortunate enough to have been given, once in my life, a present that was everything one person had to give . . . a present so incredible that it had to be wrapped in a full moon.

*With my old friend Bob Petersen. I forgot
what we were shooting—probably anything.*

○ *JUST OUT OF REACH*

THE FIELDS I have grazed in with the most lasting pleasure have been flowered with grouse and woodcock. I visit some of them every year about this time, but many now only in memory; housing developments and paved roads have covered up those alder runs and the meandering paths of soft-eyed Holsteins.

I try to resist the idea of "breaking in" new bird covers. The old covers were as familiar as my bedroom. I knew where to get a drink of cool water, where to find a comfortable place to sit and rest, and just where the late afternoon breezes were most likely to blow. There were always two or three places that held birds when they were in the cover; if those hot spots were empty, I'd move on without wasting too much time. I had other things to look for in my old coverts. There might be a bee tree, a small bed of lady slippers, or a white birch leaning at the perfect angle to rest against.

A new cover is strangeness itself. You enter it with a mixture of excitement and a feeling of not really belonging. Whatever discovery you do make might not really be what you are looking for at all—it might not fit. A new cover might not have that magic mixture of old apples and aspens and ferns and birches. The spring, if there is one, can remain hidden for years. One of my old covers had a small bubbling spring that my father had shown me. Left on my own, I would have never have found it and would have missed the pleasure of scooping back the side to the shape of a large teacup and, when the water, cleared, having a long, tooth-hurting drink.

Then I'd stand back and watch the dog dig the spring a little deeper and wider before she'd shove her face in the mud with so much obvious pleasure I could catch myself saying "ahhh" in her behalf.

You have to *wear* a new cover for a few seasons, breaking it in like a pair of boots. You have to experiment with times of day in new cover. In an old, familiar cover, you knew whether it held birds in the morning, the late afternoon, or in special cases, almost any time of the day.

One of my favorite old covers was too thick to shoot or work a dog in, but it always held birds if the flights were down. We would pull our hats down over our eyes, put our hands up in front of our faces, and wade around flushing birds out. The birds would drop into a neighboring section and after letting them settle down for a while, we'd go in there with the dogs and shotguns. I'm not sure I'd disturb a resting cover like that now—I might do it once a season, especially if I had a puppy to fool with. I appreciate more than I used to the need for a quiet place to collect oneself.

A new cover doesn't have that special sense of personal history. You can't point to the patch of mountain laurel where Lefty made his first holding point on a grouse. That happened a long time ago . . . I walked in behind the dog and the bird cut right behind that big cedar just as I shot—see how that one branch is kind of short and raggedy—and Lefty just turned around and gave me that cockeyed stare he had from that brown patch around his eye. I swear he wanted to laugh but didn't know how!

It's hard to predict what a particular bird will do in a particular cover until you get to know the lay of the land—where the birds will hold and where they won't in certain kinds of weather. It takes time to learn when the berries will be plentiful, if the spring is drying up, or if a fox or owl has moved in. You have to live in a new cover yourself to see who your neighbors are and what the economy is doing.

Of course old covers change, but you can see that from one year to the next, and of course you can tell by checking the nesting in the summer season. If the cover is getting a little too grassy or thick, you could ask Mr. Jeffers about running a few of his guernseys in there for a while. You might even do a little clearing by hand, or just let it go and see what happens. There's always lightning or drought, or just plain old age. It's not too hard to check a cover's pulse every now and then, listening for the drumming of a grouse or the thin, reedy song of a spiraling woodcock.

Discovering a new cover is good for us. I find that I get like an old dog myself, working a familiar spot as you would a routine opening—go in as far as the old apple tree, then hurry to the spring run, and so forth. I know I should be hunting to see if the cover has changed, but too often I slide through as if I were on a game farm looking for planted birds where the orange ribbons are. Working someplace new reminds us that gunners ought to know as much as their bird dogs do about cover.

Of course, if you're lucky, a new cover can become timeless to you. It has offered you its secret places and you take them as your right. You enter *here* with loving curiosity, introducing the dog as gently as you can to the corner where the three or four woodcock are scattered like hidden surprises. You take one, feeling pride and regret as you hold it, mouth-wet, and slide it in your vest.

Then there will be an afternoon when you feel a strange misgiving about an old cover you have come a long way to visit. Something is askew, something is changed in an almost ominous way. Then it comes to you. The evergreens you remember as just about right for a Christmas cutting are now towering giants throwing long shadows that close out the light. There is no warming from the sun and the sudden chilling of the breeze is almost frightening. You wonder who is the hunted here as you call the dog in to walk beside you. The way out to the open meadow seems overly long.

A cover is more than just a place where birds are. I know that a cover bereft of birds is just vegetation. But a corner of a field that is likely to hold a covey of quail, or a berry thicket that reeks of birdiness, gives an incredible life and excitement to a place that would be meaningless unless you were a hunter. Part of it is the satisfaction of being enough of a hunter to guess right more often than not—following a deep instinct and having it work. It's the difference between just walking through the wild or being a part of it, the difference between being a hunter or a spectator—the difference between looking *for* something or *at* something.

Almost every year I see a cover that I *know* is perfect. It has the perfect colors—the olive of aspen, the green of spruce—and, pushing the cover, the light, damp smell of a valley waiting for winter. Yet when I go in, it's like knocking at a friend's door and knowing instantly there is no one home. Then, almost every year I fool around in the most unlikely places and find nothing I'm looking for—except birds.

All of which proves, as any of my dogs could have told me, that I'm not as smart as I'd like to think I am. Maybe I ought to face up to the fact that the hunter I want to be is like the perfect cover I've always been looking for—just out of reach.

○ *MESSAGE FROM A PICKLE JAR*

IN ONE CORNER of my little office is a large ceramic jar about 18 or 20 inches high. I know it once served as a vessel for making sauerkraut or homemade pickles but its career has been downgraded; now it holds my assortment of fly rods.

When fishermen start collecting, we tend to buy rods that are either too cheap or too expensive. The cheap rods are to learn with; the good ones are put away until we know we have some sort of handle on the whole operation. We tell ourselves we'll give away the beginners' stuff to one of the acolytes we'll run across, but we almost never do. Once acquired, a fly rod takes on another dimension; however slim, it will have a history and it can whisper a message when we slide it from its tube.

As luck would have it, I acquired early on a few rods made by one or another of the apostles. But when some Beaverkill bard asks, "What's that thing you're using?" I can reply, with total honesty: "I went out in such a hurry this morning that I left my Paul Young and the Payne standing by the door!" This is the immaculate truth for that's where my old rod jar stands—by the door. I am fishing with a near nameless rod (French, of all things . . .) because I think I cast better with it and because it was given to me by an old friend as as encouragement to get me started in fly fishing. When I use it I am immediately both younger and happier, as when large flagons of white wine brought streamside euphoria instead of indigestion.

Like most fishermen I have favorite rods that rebel against logic. I am not one of those who doesn't use something for fear it will get scratched or nicked; I prefer stuff that has seen a bit of use. But I am not a person who takes the greatness of a rod on faith. I have two or three very expensive rods that bear the signature of one of the legends, and I think they're pathetic, slow, weepy rods that we put up with until something better comes along. I have a few others that are just the opposite—exhausting to such an extent that the thought of using them makes me tired. I keep them out of some strange tradition and the fact that no one else really wants them either. But they do lend a little prestige to my old pickle jar.

Every so often I like to rummage around in the corner jar and pull out a rod. I piece it together and begin endangering my fluorescent lights with the tip. For a minute or two I am back in a long canoe on the Restigouche, watching a Dusty Miller or a Roger's Fancy run through Chain-of-Rocks pool. The swirl and then the feel of the line going slack are as vivid as usual; and I can clearly hear the guide say, "Thirty-five if he's an ounce!"

I have the Henry's Fork 24-inch rainbow rod, a longer rod that went to Iceland with me, and my 15-foot, two-handed salmon rod for the never-to-be trip to Norway. My favorite? The one I can't wait to take outside? The newest rod in my pickle jar, of course—the one I've never used!

After the leaves are down, fishermen tend to tune out for a time. A man wandering around in a tackle shop or leafing idly through a wish book in late fall doesn't need physical additions to his storehouse; he is probably looking for a peaceful place to rest his mind a minute. He needs to step into the Chapel of Our Brothers of the Angle. In time he is refreshed, and he can again cope for a while with the bothersome affairs that fill the time between rivers. But he has to leave something, so he lights a candle by ordering some Adams in numbers 12 and 14 and perhaps a new pair of clippers for his vest. He has looked at the rods and seen what's new in the reels, but he doesn't need them yet; someday, but not now.

A more serious mood is most likely to strike a fisherman in mid-winter. He wonders if he shouldn't be spending more time with his wife in the garden, come summer. He knows he's been neglecting the house and yard and he wonders if he's really spending too much time tying flies, and limiting his reading to Wright, Nemes, and Schwiebert. When the moment is this dark, nothing less than a new reel or a pair of stocking-foot waders can halt the movement toward reform.

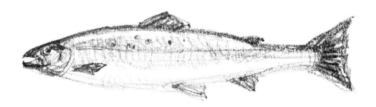

The most serious crisis can occur almost any time, but it's most dangerous just before fishing season. The first sign is a strange lassitude—sporting catalogues are tossed, unread, into the magazine pile, garage sales of known fellow anglers are ignored, the TU dinner is forgotten, and the money saved for a new WF7F is spent on a rake or spade.

Fortunately, one learns from one's errors. It has been said that the loudest voice of the revival meeting is raised by the man who won't or can't change his ways. So it is that the man who had publicly quit fishing as a childish waste of time is most likely the man who has a new emergency rod, so far unused. In many case, there are two such rods, both 12-weights for tarpon. I have, in the past, also had emergency salmon rods built and one "cure-all"—a wisp of bamboo that struggles with a three-weight line unless the air is still and the surface of the pool is a mirror. I have seen the error of my ways.

I don't want to lay too heavy a burden on fishing. I am not siding with those who would put an old Kosmic reel or a Gillum rod on a level with relics of the True Cross. Fishing is a private escape. Some are cleansed by standing in 40-degree water and flinging leadcore shooting heads across steelhead rivers. Others, no doubt less troubled, can face their wives and children after only a few hours of drifting a hopper or a caddis over Snake River rainbows. And some fishermen, more saintly to start with, can manage a smile just *thinking* about panfish, or poppers and bass ponds.

A day of fishing is never a waste. The oldtimers know that although cooperation by the fish is the icing, there's plenty that can stick with the cake—trying out a new rod or reel, or a pair of waders, or watching, always with the feeling of seeing a miracle, feeding fish making little diamonds on the surface of the stream.

Think of this. You are on a brook or lake where you fished some years ago. There, across the little feeder stream, is the same muskrat house. You hear the old, mysterious conversation between frogs and the scolding of redwing blackbirds. A strange feeling comes over you; everything is still the way it always was when you fished here last. Then you realize that as long as you fish here, nothing will ever change.

○ THE ANNUAL REPORT I

Standing behind the lectern is a man 6 feet tall. You might notice first his soft but piercing eyes, the carriage of the born athlete, and the presence so often called "commanding." The trained observer might notice other things as well—the once powerful body now humbled by too much yard work and household chores; the once singular mind now teetering on the edge of rationality from the tension and erosion created from trying to raise two daughters. But the pride is still there and it's almost tangible. Dressed in a now-shabby shooting coat, he is shuffling through some notes with one hand; the other hand is placed in front of his necktie as if he were trying to conceal a few moth holes.

At the edge of the stage, close to the exit, a tall blonde woman is smoothing the wrinkles from a blanket placed on the floor, while a rather pudgy yellow Labrador watches patiently. Once the dog has settled down, the blonde dumps a bag of what appears to be salmon flies in her lap. As the speaker clears his throat, she begins to sort the colorful flies according to size and pattern, pausing now and then to touch a small file to a hook point. At last the man begins to speak.

FIRST, I'D LIKE to express my appreciation for your attendance at the presentation of the annual report. Rather than bore you with an uninteresting recitation of dollars and cents, I will briefly outline how the corporation has fared; specific questions about profit and loss will be answered at the conclusion of the meeting.

One would hope that in our burgeoning economy we would find the corporation swept along in the boom. Unfortunately, this isn't quite the case. But there is some good news that I'm delighted to share with you. A case of 12-gauge field loads that we thought had been stolen turned up during the cleaning of a closet in my office! We were looking for a pair of insulated waders, which surprisingly were found on the same day in the same place, a bit worse for wear after the mice got to them; they must be replaced as soon as times are a little more prosperous. The Chairman has been using this as an excuse for the replacement of the old family cat, ignoring the fact that the mouse nest we found was indisputably made out of what appears to be cat hair.

I have compromised and placed the loss of the waders under "natural acts."

Under found objects, you will notice a barrel for an 870 Remington, a gun which for some reason I do not own. I hastily pointed out to the Chairman that the Corporation ought to take advantage of this little bonanza and purchase an 870, but my suggestion has been countered by hers to sell the barrel. I consider her remark to have been made in unthinking haste and have placed the barrel (30-inch, Mod.) under assets.

Also found was an 8-foot fly rod for an 8-weight line—the rod turned up when the Chairman made her annual expedition to the youngest daughter's bedroom. The discovery canceled a pending purchase order for such a rod, and I see no harm in listing this windfall under *profits*. The Chairman speaks of this as false accounting—I leave it to you. But when Labor leans over backwards to appease Management and is only answered with scorn, how can Management expect harmony?

Under *loss,* again in dispute with Management, I list an unopened carton of chewing tobacco, which disappeared from my private refrigerator. I have my suspicions, but I have remained silent. We are also missing a brown shooting sweater, and following a heated discussion of whether or not the garment was left at the dry cleaners by Management or left at a gun club by Labor, it was decided to let the matter pass for the time being.

A new trap gun has been acquired on loan (Management please note!), but the expected improvement from the 16 yard line has been slow in coming. However, this trifling item might appear on

Why is this man not smiling? I have just missed high eight to lose the club skeet championship. I have also lost it missing low five and low six, among others.

next year's acquisitions list, so I see no reason to debate the issue until sometime in the future. Also problematical is the purchase of a new lightweight field gun (28 gauge, Mod. & Full). A doctor I shoot with has recommended a 6-pound gun in deference to my health, but since Management scoffs, saying that I need more exercise, not less, this matter has also been postponed. I only hope, for her sake, that the consequences aren't dire. She might never be able to forgive herself!

On a different note, the Canadian salmon trip was somewhat of a disappointment. The river was low and few of the traditional pools produced any fish; consequently, the annual salmon dinner has been postponed. An antelope hunt was no more successful. Again, uncommon weather might have been a factor, since high winds caused two otherwise sure shots to come up empty . . . .

We did have a few geese, some doves, and a smattering of pheasants for the table, but so far, our ability to "live off the land" has rightly been called into question. Management has insisted on cost accounting travel, licenses, shells, and miscellaneous, and has remarked (joking, of course) that we could have lived on caviar and champagne and been way ahead. Why she says this (knowing I don't care too much for caviar) escapes me, unless it's the usual weak feminine attempt at irony.

The farm has produced more than three dozen Canada geese and at least six sets of fawns. I also see a handful of pheasants where recently there had been none. The big brown-and-white doe has not come back into the front meadow and the Canada with the crooked leg failed to return to her old nesting place on the island in the pond. One of the old willows has died, but the experiment with bald-kneed cypress has come along quite well. I find that I am largely content with the great plan that "giveth and taketh away."

I find it difficult to report that we have lost Maggie to a speeding car. It was her habit to sometimes sit at the head of the lane when I was away, and I took immense pleasure in seeing her there, waiting, when I came home. I would blow the horn and she would bark and race me down the lane where we would wrestle for a minute, and then she would go back into my office and sit on her bed by my typewriter. She was a thoughtful and helpful companion to me, and her ability to keep the evil Despair at a distance will be sorely missed. It's been such a long time that I haven't had her for comfort that I had forgotten how hard, sometimes, it is to be alone.

As the speaker turns his back on the audience, the blonde lady stands, picks up the blanket from the floor, and shakes it gently, sending a small cloud of light-colored dog hair to settle on the speaker's clothes. It seems to comfort him.

*This is Judy, one of the best dogs I ever had.
She was a little high strung, but then ladies of quality
often are. She would often cry when I left her to
hunt with one of my other dogs and more than once I
turned the car around and came back to get her.
Once when she lost a litter of puppies she went to my
daughter's room and gathered half a dozen stuffed
animals to her swollen breasts; few things I've ever seen
have touched me as deeply. Often dogs become lost in
time, but not Judy, she is still in my mind as clear
and magical as a shooting star.*

○ LABRADOR LEGENDS

I'VE BEEN DOING a little research on the Labrador retriever recently and thought I'd pass on some information of more than common interest. Chances are excellent that none of your dog-owning friends have run across these little-known tidbits of fact, so not only can you have some fun (the best kind is always at the expense of a good friend), but their estimation of your intelligence could go up a notch or two, a rare opportunity for most of us!

The Lab was originally bred to dig up bulbs in flower gardens. It was only after this trait was genetically sealed into its nature that the notion of "off season" work first occurred to its early breeders, who were also, by good fortune, dedicated waterfowlers.[1]

In the old days Labs were confined at night in small rooms—later known as "sheds"—from which their hair was collected at regular intervals. The hair was used to stuff church cushions, sofa pillows, and the like—things where economy rather than comfort was the primary aim. A normal-size Lab, about 70 to 80 pounds, will shed twice its weight in hair every year. Curiously, a *reversal* in the color of backgrounds often increases this process. It is a known fact that if you keep a black Lab in an area where the primary colors are light, it will shed more; yellow Labs do the opposite. The early handlers learned to wear light-colored jackets, thus encouraging black Labs to shed even more profusely. Furniture placed in these rooms covered in pale and dark fabrics also produced the optimum amount of hair.

Tippy, Judy and Pitsy. Vain, willful and perfectly aware that I was put on Earth to spoil them—and vice versa.

The Lab has a natural instinct to seek dark places and to lie immobile in them. Top government officials spent $1.4 million in secret research, using black Labs to lie in dark hallways in some of the most sensitive parts of the Pentagon complex, knowing that intruders who bypassed the electronic surveillance system would trip over the dogs, causing them to bark and thereby summoning guards. The project, which showed great initial promise, was finally abandoned because the computers could not be screened from the fine Lab hair; it was claimed that on the average, each Lab caused more than $200 worth of damage semiannually to carpeting and rugs.

Most behavioral scientists agree that the fairly recent development of the Frisbee brought out the full potential of the Labrador. A few others claim it was the golf ball. My own dogs favored vollleyballs when golf balls were no longer obtainable, but these were undoubtedly isolated incidents.[2]

There is still disagreement on why Labradors chew so much printed matter—books, magazines, newspapers, etc. One group believes it's the wood pulp content of paper that triggers their latent instinct to dig bulbs, carry limbs, and gnaw the corners of doors and cabinets. Another faction believes that the breed is trying to imitate a human behavior—reading—and chews in an effort to please us. I hope it's the former and not the latter. I don't mind Maggie rolling an eye occasionally at my shooting, but I wouldn't want her criticizing my writing. I swear that I have seen her smile at an Ed Zern column, although I doubt if she understands more than half of what he writes; I have the feeling that she associates him with lost golf balls.

Did you know that a Labrador cannot attain its full growth potential without frequent contact with metal wire? Tearing a hole in chain-link kennel fencing seems to be the most potent growth aid, but close behind are running through screen doors, garden fencing, and chicken wire. If a Lab is deprived of these opportunities, it will seek alternatives such as teething on metal table legs, shoe eyelets, electrical cord, etc. A Lab pup's first food dish, according to the Richard Wolters Institute, should be metal—a pie plate, sauce pan, or similar container. Later, you move up to so-called "indestructible" plastic or ceramic dishes.

We all know that Labradors are somewhat disposed to having a swim. But I bet you didn't know they prefer to dry themselves by friction rather than shaking. The favored material for drying is wallpaper, followed closely by upholstery, including car seats, and then ordinary clothing—pant legs, skirts, hunting coats, etc. In-depth tests prove conclusively that Labs know air drying leads to split ends and a rough coat. Is this one of the influences of TV?

One of the least understood traits of the Labrador is a dislike of "theater," as the scientists phrase it. What they mean by this is that a Lab will almost always work better for you alone than when you have other people with you. I think we've all seen this behavior trait and never recognized it for what it really is—a form of canine shyness. Once you explain this to your duck hunting buddies, I'm sure they'll understand why the great retrieves you've bragged about don't happen when they're around. It's no different than asking you to stand up and make a speech to a crowd.

Another eye opener for me was discovering what sounds are the most exciting to a Lab. I'll bet you always thought the most exciting sound was a shotgun, right? Well, that sound happens to be

well down on the list. A series of tests was conducted to judge a Lab's reaction to various sounds. Favorites, in the order of attraction, were as follows: opening a refrigerator door, a game involving a ball (golf, softball, catch, etc.), the click of a fly reel, cracking nuts, making popcorn, unwrapping a sandwich or a candy bar, and splitting kindling.

Obviously I have only scratched the surface of the delightful history of the Labrador retriever. Once-sacred beliefs, now shattered, litter my workroom floor as I unearth more strange facts. I will continue to dig (sorry) until truth about hunting dogs stands unblemished before us.

Just a hint of what's to come:

Astonishingly, the word *setter* doesn't derive from this breed's habit of sitting after scenting a gamebird, but from its amusing habit of stretching out, full length on a popular piece of early Victorian furniture—the settee. Those of you who fancy yourselves scholars will see the link between the "EE" (the one receiving the action) and the "ER," the perpetrator. It's exciting work as you can see, and as soon as the ice fishing season is over, I'll be back with more!

[1]One such waterfowler was an early Dutch settler in the area of New Rochelle, N.Y., whose name was either Zurn or Zern—scholars disagree on the exact spelling—and who trained his Lab to dig up moles in the garden as well as bulbs. In his only known note on this, he insisted that if a good cat be called a "ratter," why not call his dog a "molar."

[2]The phrase "having a ball' is now believed to be a corruption of "halving a ball." It's amazing how obvious some things are when explained. Labs who like to chew things have made some other terms popular as well, but this is not the place to review them.

One of my favorite places in the world—the Restigouche River in Quebec. Obviously one of my better days; I'd guess about 14 for one and about 10 or 12 for the other. On the other hand, maybe they're a bit better than that!

○ A DIAMOND AMONG EMERALDS

I'VE OFTEN THOUGHT of doing a little book about the places I'd like to be every year, month by month. Of course, the possibilities of actually being in these places are almost nonexistent because such travels would depend on justice and mercy, which seem to be almost nonexistent as well.

June is one of the easier months to pick an ideal location because at this time there is little in the way of shooting to conflict with fishing, and since the intention of this whole idea is to investigate the ideal, the supreme, the *sine qua non*, we can also assume that money and connections are no object. That being so, I will choose the best fishing for Atlantic salmon on Canada's three legendary rivers—the Grand Cascapedia, the Restigouche, and the Moise.

There is little to choose between these three "big fish" rivers. Each turns up a 40-pound class fish every summer and each produces rambling tales of fish seen, hooked, and lost that are estimated as high as 60 pounds. The record fish on the Grand Cascapedia is 54 pounds. The record on the Moise, I believe, is still 45 pounds. I don't know what the record is on the Restigouche, since there are several different camps and associations, and no official body that looks after the whole river. I do know of a fish taken in 1959 that weighed 50 pounds, so size is a standoff when comparing these rivers. However, if sheer poundage were the final tipping of favor, I'd choose the Grand Cascapedia or the Moise over the Restigouche, but not with any total conviction.

All three rivers are substantial pieces of water fished from "Gaspe" boats—locally made canoes that run about 22 feet or a bit longer. None of the rivers have any wading water to speak of, but I'm almost as excited about a day on the river with one of the great boatmen as I am about the fishing.

It is the character of these three great salmon rivers that differentiates one from another. Much of the Moise is best described as *awesome*. One steeply pitched stretch that I ran looked like a down staircase, and the sight of an abandoned canoe bent double on a rock did nothing to change my mind about the Moise not being a river to take lightly. The Grand Cascapedia also has memorable stretches only a bit less steep. But on the Restigouche, you find no brawling rapids, no long runs where you sit watching the guide handle the pole like the artist he really is, nimbly tucking the bow here and there around giant rocks with as much calm as a lady knitting a sweater cuff.

The Restigouche is a river that asks you to meditate—to look upon it with thoughtful study as it runs deep and clear, sparkling like a diamond set among emeralds. As Dean Sage notes in his magnificent book, *The Restigouche and Its Salmon Fishing*, "It's a noble stream, with no falls or rapids in its whole course that a canoe cannot surmount. Its numerous winding and abrupt turns, so favorable for forming good salmon pools, also give a variety and choice of beautiful scenery which is rare to find on any river."

We will fish here on the Restigouche. Our choice is only slightly more than arbitrary; I have fished the Restigouche and know it better than the other two rivers. And I am always anxious to go back. I anxiously await the first long look at the river from the great heights of the Matapedia bridge; it is a look as special as laying eyes on an old and dear friend that I have not seen for years.

Unlike many of the small salmon rivers, the Restigouche can call on you to perform with a sizable piece of terminal iron. In the old days 8/0 flies, often called Dee irons, were not only legal but common. These wise words are from Charles Phair's book, *Atlantic Salmon Fishing*: "If I were going to buy only one salmon rod, it would most certainly be a two-handed rod, and thirteen feet in length . . . thirteen feet because that is large enough for any of the big rivers, and a large wet fly can be thrown with it (I do not say cast)."

That was written in 1937, and although I don't lament the pass-

Another favorite place—Iceland. This is a couple of years later than the picture in Quebec but I'm wearing the same hat. Hats are like favorite flies, if they work you never change them or lose them, hopefully.

ing of the thrill that goes with pitching 8/0 flies, I think that the loss of the two-handed rod is a mistake. I will bring mine as I have before. It's a 14-foot graphite Bruce & Walker, made in England, and takes an 11-weight double-taper line. I never leave home without it. My other favorite, the one that really gets the workout, is a 9-foot Orvis Powerflex for a 9-weight line; I find it both powerful enough to throw a long fly into a wind and delicate enough to use with dries. I use several lines with it—a floater and different-rate sink tips. For normal wet fly fishing, I have come to like the intermediate; its slow sink rate and ease of casting are hard to fault.

Most of the best water on the Restigouche is under the control of the Restigouche Club—which is good for both the salmon and the river. There is very little public water, which, while inconvenient, has helped keep the salmon stocks as strong as they are, so

Relaxing in a salmon camp. This is in sub-arctic Canada which explains the refreshments (doesn't it?). I was not alone.

we'll have to make the assumption that we are guests of the Club and that the members have offered us our choice of pools!

Up the river about 30 miles from the Bay de Chaleur is another branch river called the Patapedia. The quality of the fishing where the Patapedia flows into the Restigouche is so extraordinary that the water is known as the Million Dollar Pool. I have drifted over this pool in a canoe on a downriver journey and seen banks of salmon, stacks of salmon, rafts of salmon, with their noses pressed into the clean cold water rushing into the big river from the Patapedia. We will fish here.

It's your turn to cast, and conditions are perfect. There's a little upstream breeze, and when the sun comes out from behind the scattered clouds, we can see a line of salmon down below us restlessly rolling like a chain of hammered silver.

We will take one salmon each—borrow them really—and then put them back where they belong. To do more would be like prying the jewels from a crown. The river has given us two salmon and we have given them back. We feel pleased with ourselves.

On the way back down the river, past the almost too perfect lodges designed by Sanford White (who also created the Night Hawk fly), we see salmon rolling everywhere—pulled and pushed by the same urgent sparks shared by us all, to reproduce our kind while we are still strong and wild.

The early moonlight seems even more magical than usual. Before we leave this Restigouche I want to take a picture, a last impression. I will stand and wait for a salmon to roll loudly, right there by that bend, so he will then disappear from sight like a friend turning a corner, with the promise of seeing him again still hanging on the evening air.

These snow geese and I met in the highlands of Mexico. A remote and wild place far from their arctic nesting, I never will stop wondering about this sort of distant journey nor what strange impulses brought us together.

○ *JUNK JEWELRY*

SEVERAL OF THE GEESE attendant on my pond, many of them year-round residents, are wearing large yellow plastic neck collars. On the collars are numbers large enough to be read at a distance of 100 yards through ordinary binoculars. The local fish and game people tell me the collars are part of a study involving resident and nonresident geese.

In my simple way, I asked what they needed to know about Canada geese that required these atrocious neckbands, or to put it even more simply, who cares? I got an evasive answer. When I called in a number from one of my geese, which was sitting on the lawn about 20 feet from where I'm writing this, the girl who answered the telephone said, "We don't handle that," and told me to call another number. I said if it was all that important to have these bands reported, I'd leave my telephone number and the interested official could call me back. "It doesn't work that way," I was told. I replied that as far as I was concerned, it doesn't work at all.

I may be wrong about the need for the proliferation of uncomfortable looking plastic collars on my geese, the radio collars on our bears, and similar devices harnessed to various other creatures—there are even tiny transmitters stuffed in the bowels of snakes. But I'm more and more convinced that it is the existence of such devices that dictates their use rather than a need to learn about the movements of bears or to reaffirm that geese will fly here and there for fresh grass and clean water.

No doubt some good accrues from all this labeling and transmission; at least it keeps food on the table for a number of wildlife biologists. But I suspect that it is the old adage of "knowing more than we can handle" that continues to haunt us.

We've all sat through countless hours of so-called "nature" films watching as some poor beast is pursued by helicopter or truck until some aspiring Ph.D. finally injects it with what is hopefully a nonlethal dose of drugs in order to take its temperature and commit other almost indecent inquiries into its private life. I fight the urge to stand up in my dark little room and shout, "Why are you doing all this?" I have listened carefully to the explanations and little of it makes any sense. There is, I suppose, the cheap drama of man sticking his nose into an area where it does little good except to expand his already overweened vanity.

The sight of a moose—an animal that seems to have a look of perpetual wonderment and questioning—wearing a great fluorescent plastic necklace with an electronic tattletale pendant is an embarrassment to mankind, an indiginity to both man and beast. If such an animal needs to be observed night and day, why not extend the spirit of "fair chase" and have somebody go out, night and day, and observe it?

I have nothing against scientific observation, census, or even plain curiosity. I am as interested as the next ignoramus about the curious life cycle of the migrating butterfly or the whereabouts of the black-footed ferrets, but I think there are some technological gadgets that we could resist in the name of decency, even if life is a little more incomplete without them.

If I sound like a voice from the past fighting against progress and enlightenment, I don't mean to remain ignorant or to insist that the world is flat. It's just that I'm more than a little annoyed at seeing wildlife drugged into senselessness, and collared and tagged, or whatever, like a prize Cheviot or Charolais.

The biologists, when I corner one long enough to make my annoying speech, answer me with their scientific equivalent of "You can't make an omelet without breaking eggs." And it usually ends, as do most arguments, with neither of us listening to what the other has to say. They tell me what great things they have accomplished, and while I applaud some of it, I strongly suspect that a lot of the rodeoing and labeling is not really productive. It may be interesting to be involved in, but is it really adding to our body of knowledge?

I wish that whoever had the idea of a giant neckband had thought a little harder and come up with a model that would have fallen off after a couple of months, rather than the one that seems to be more permanent than most wedding rings. Some wildlife managers asked me last year if they could come to my ponds and band more geese when they're in the molt. I told them no, but I did offer to help them take off the bands already in place.

Before you accuse me of trying to return to the Stone Age, you should understand that several wildlife people I know well also see little point in most of this branding and draping of wild things.

One of these professionals was involved in rousting a bear from its hibernation last winter. Among other "important" things, they checked the radio collar. Underneath that cinch was a belt of raw and angry skin.

"How did that make you feel?" I asked the man.

"Like I had just seen someone throw a stone through a church window," he answered.

*In the foreground, a 24-pound salmon.
In the background a 200-pound salmon
fisherman and Iceland.*

○ *THE REEL THING*

I DOUBT there's a much better equipped fly fisherman in the country. To see me standing there, in full fig, you'd have to be impressed. I have a decent rod, the best waders I know of, and the usual wretched excess of impedimenta including scissors, clippers, forceps, and a variety of unguents and oils hanging off me like ornaments on a Christmas tree. The reel I'm using might not be the most expensive one you can buy, what with the rush of big ticket newcomers on the market, but it will be a "best," as they say about some of the old London shotguns.

From the very beginning, I have been captivated by fly reels. Most of my reels aren't all that rare, but they do offer the ephemeral combination of design and function called quality. The theory often expressed is that a fly reel is merely a line holder, and I have no argument, especially when one is fishing for trout smaller than 20 inches. But there's no reason I know of why a line holder shouldn't be pleasing to the eye and the hand and the ear.

When you move up a notch to big trout, or salmon, it's my opinion that the qualities of a reel are critical. The drag must be perfect, the capacity for backing in excess of adequate, the weight ideal to balance and "work" the rod. The construction must be strong enough to take an unavoidable knock, but without making the reel unduly heavy and tiring. Even the click of a reel is important. It ought to be a clear and thrilling counterpoint to the sounds of the river, exciting the mind like a musical crescendo as the fish runs with urgent speed, and as clear and distinct as a clock ticking toward midnight when the duel is over and the net is near.

The reels I have squandered my welfare checks on are centered around some Walkers, a few early Hardy's, and two or three antiques that are English but bear no makers' names—I just like the way they're made. My bigger rods are outfitted with the unparalleled Bogdan and the classic, understated beauty and reliability of VomHofe and Zwarg. I would love to own an old Hardy Cascapedia, but every collector ought to have something to keep searching for.

Envious friends have seen fit to mention that it might be possible to get by with less, or fewer. No doubt I could live without the odd glass of single malt Scotch I enjoy on special occasions, but I fail to see how it would make me a better person. There is my practical side, which certain loved ones tend to make light of. No intelligent salmon fisherman would ever be without a floating line, a sink-tip line, and intermediate density line, and a couple of variations of all those. It just happens that I have them on separate reels. The defense rests.

I saw an old Hardy salmon reel in a little village shop in Scotland a few years ago and I went in and asked the shopkeeper about it. He took the reel out of the case, and when I admired it to excess, I think he came up with a "rich American" price. I remarked that it was a bit dear. He admitted that and said that it was also a bit rare and I admitted I knew that as well. It's no thrill to pay an excessive price for anything you collect, no matter how much you want to own it, and I'm a bit Scotch myself, so I merely thanked him and left.

But after two days I had succeeded in rationalizing ownership by the methods we all use: I'll never find one like it again, it will only cost more later on, I'll skip supper for a couple of days, etc., etc. With that struggle over I marched back to the shop, handed the owner a pile of pounds, and said I'd come back for the old reel.

The man pushed the money back and said he'd decided he'd rather keep the reel; he'd had it so long he'd gotten fond of looking at it. I told him that I understood perfectly, but that someday I'd come back to see if he'd changed his mind. The next year I was back to fish there was a new owner and the old reel was gone. I asked what had happened to the reel and he said it was one of the few things the previous owner had insisted on taking with him. As you might have guessed, the reel was a Cascapedia—in near mint condition.

Normally the British are casual to indifferent about their tackle. It's sort of a reverse snobbery—"one leaves that sort of decision to the shopkeeper. . . . " I know a couple of very avid salmon fishermen in Great Britain who still use their well-worn grandfather's rods and reels and who each tie on a March Brown or a Monro Killer and leave it on the leader (sorry, the *cast*) until they lose it or the season ends. They aren't very curious about tackle, but they do feel that our one-handed salmon rods are silly and inadequate and that we carry too much junk with us on the river. I enjoy using their big two-handed rods and I carry too much junk on the river, so for me it's a trade-off.

I was in another shop in Scotland, in Brora, buying some small salmon doubles that I like—size 12's and 14's. While I was talking with the proprietor about reels, the conversation got around to the Bogdan. I had a Bogdan with me and I showed it to him. I demonstrated the smoothness of the drag and with an excess of zeal and pride in such fine American workmanship, I told him how much it was worth. He handed it back to me without another word, but I knew he was thinking that anyone who knew anything about salmon fishing would never need to spend that much for a reel; it would be wrong. I tried to describe the size and force of some of our rivers. I told him how big some of our salmon run, and we fish with different rods, but he had tuned out. I paid for my flies and took my leave, implying that he didn't know as much about salmon as he thought he did, and that the Scots didn't invent them. As I walked out of the store, a neat wading staff with a carved horn handle in the shape of a salmon caught my eye. I turned to go back in and ask the price, but the man had put the CLOSED sign on the door and disappeared into the back room.

This is about the time of the year when I take out the old reels and clean them up. It's a pleasant little ritual and so far I've only disabled two reels by taking them apart. Both were quickly fixed by people who knew what they were doing. Of an afternoon in the dead of winter, the click of the reel as I spin the handle conjures up a great day as warmly as it can offer the promise of the greatest season of all—the one to come.

It's entirely possible that my devotion to fly fishing has been at least partially responsible for my never having been nominated as Husband of the Year.

I'm not the kind of man who spends Sunday morning washing and polishing the family car. So when the time comes for me to go to the Great Home Pool, I can fairly assume that the Widow Hill will get the lion's a share of attention from friends who are more interested in the disposition of my Bogdans, Walkers, and Vom-Hofes than they are in my favorite chamois and wheel brush.

○ *A BIRD IN THE BUSH*

NOT FAR FROM my house, maybe a mile or so, there is a woodcock singing ground. It pleases me that woodcock gather there on their way north, thinking about romance and impatiently waiting for the evening star. I find that the courtship of the woodcock is one of the most magic and wondrous things I know—these little birds asking the essential question of the night with their tiny piping song.

It grieves me that the watchers and counters of the woodcock, especially along the Eastern coast, report that these great gamebirds are severely threatened. I have no doubt about it. My old coverts are breeding tract houses, and the once tortuous dirt roads that made it necessary to use chains on my Model A are now covered with macadam. The little brooks along which I once ran unsuccessful traplines have been drained, and where I used to walk through aspens and birches, I now find lawns with ceramic deer and plastic ducks, proving, I suppose, that the residents love wildlife.

Woodcock are unique in their attraction to the upland sportsman. They come and go in charming mystery surrounded by legends and lore, and their supposed kinship to the dictates of the moon seems as fitting as any. Finding good woodcock cover was and still is among the most secret of all treasure hunts. When I was a boy and Bill or Emmett held up a string of 'cock for your envy, no one over the age of ten would even dream of asking the great question, "Where?" Secret swamps and meadow runs were handed down from father to son like their old Parkers and Smiths, and where a good covert was known to be someone's, either by ownership or precedent, it was usually left alone. Not always, but usually.

I still mark the beginning of bird season by the first woodcock I see bobbing in the dusking flight around sundown in late September. In its quiet magic, this single bird tolls the time of the year as majestically as the chorus of a thousand geese. In years past, the arrival of what we wrongly called "the flight" would send me into a frenzy of travel—if that's an apt phrase for a kid who carried his

single-shot 20-gauge across the handlebars of his bicycle or walked from damp spot to damp spot trying to think like a long-billed bird searching for earthworms.

When I graduated to our Model A, it was the same thing, only in wider circles. I was led from covert to covert by rumor, speculation, wild guessing, and a little local knowledge flavored by what I had read in the outdoor magazines. I usually found some birds in one place or another, hassled them with erratic wingshooting, and prized the very few I took each season way out of proportion, just like the other local gunners. Woodcock were always special.

I can still see an old orchard, a sidehill of birches and rhododendron, and a spring that always offered watercress, if nothing else.

I remember my first and only true "double" and a handful of misses that cost me some others; success in the bird field, then as ever, was always a pleasant surprise. It's a good thing I can recall those days past, since they'll never be repeated. I don't think I'll be shooting many more, if any, woodcock again, at least not along the Eastern coast.

It's the evil and dark thing we have learned to call progress; we live with it because we don't have any choice. You'll have to humor me when I want to weep over the loss of what to most people looked like a wild tangle of hazel or aspen. I drive my girls past a shopping center and remark, out of nowhere, "I used to hunt woodcock there." One of them teases me by saying, " . . . and before that there were dinosaurs and mammoths." I'm maybe a dinosaur myself, but I don't say so out loud.

This past year the woodcock season has been shortened and the bag limit reduced. Fine. It won't bring back the spring runs and the old orchards, but let's hope it will help the birds. Certainly it can't hurt. The woodcock that I might have seen flying over my fields last fall could have been under the gun earlier in New Brunswick, Maine, New Hampshire, or Pennsylvania. After leaving me the bird has to avoid pointers, setters, Britts, and whatever in Virginia, the Carolinas, Georgia, and Louisiana—with fewer and fewer places to rest and feed from start to finish.

The U.S. Fish and Wildlife Service folks, for whom I have great respect, have admitted that they don't know many answers. They have asked Eastern sportsmen to be understanding and patient with reduced seasons and lower limits, and, of course, all sportsmen are. But we also ask ourselves, "What can I do?"

Well, quite a few gunners are setting a personal limit of one or two birds, with no more than half a dozen or so for the season. Others just go out with the idea of taking two or three shots and then stopping. Some just work the dogs and don't shoot at all. I was recently in the odd position of letting a bird fly away without shooting and then having another gunner fell it. When he asked me why I hadn't shot, I just said I didn't see the 'cock. Maybe if enough of us pass up more shots we can make a difference. Anyway, it makes me feel a bit better. I don't shoot black ducks or mallard hens for the same reason.

To most of us, it doesn't make much difference whether we come home with many birds or any birds. It doesn't make much difference to the bird dog either. I've only known one or two dogs that were smart enough to keep score; luckily, none of them were mine. (Oddly, I feel better about not shooting when I could have than I feel about donating money; not only does this show something about my Scots background, it also proves that I can understand simple things more easily than roundabout ones.)

It's too bad things have come this close to the wire, but there it is and we have to live with it. When I go to the singing grounds one of these evenings and hear that urgent piping from our gallant friends, I'm going to feel pretty pleased with myself. This is an absolute case where a bird in the bush IS better than two in the hand.

○ *SOUTHERN COMFORTS*

AS FAR AS I KNOW, my family, on my mother's side, came to this country from Scotland in the late 1830's. They settled in Alabama, and some of the boys later moved to Georgia. Now let a hundred years pass. We will slide by the Civil War and not drift off into the byways with certain folk who became lawyers and others who were wanted by the law.

One hundred years later, when I was a small boy, my red-headed mother, her voice still a curious mixture of the flavor of both Scotland and Georgia, would tell me stories. Some of them were the usual stories told to the young, some were the readings of the still delightful travails of Br'er Rabbit and Mother West Wind, and some she would just make up. These were mainly stories of the South—the South she had known and, since she was orphaned at a tragically early age, the South she dreamed, with fine blooded horses, long lanes with white-painted fences, ladies who played the piano, and gentlemen who enjoyed the best of bird dogs and the finest guns.

It was to be a long time before I ever saw the South or Scotland, but in both cases it was like entering a room that was just exactly as you expected it to be—I immediately felt at home; I was at home.

No one is ever more eager to set foot across the Mason-Dixon Line than I am. The vision of soft early mornings and the sounds of gathering bird dogs blend in warmly with the easily remembered smells of cornbread, fried ham and redeye gravy, buttermilk biscuits, and the taste of coffee touched up with a whisper of chicory. So it was with this sort of thing in mind that I whispered "yes" like a soon-to-be bride when I was asked, "How about a little turkey hunting in Virginia?"

We were just south of Richmond. My belly was stretched like a drumhead with multiple helpings of fried chicken, black-eyed peas, and collards. I drifted back into my childhood and heard my mother's voice. I pleasured myself by humming snatches of "Dixie" (I am not allowed to sing unless I am alone) and sliding into a medley of songs from The War Between The States, mixed in with what little I remembered from Stephen Foster. I was a hog in the melon patch. I was not thinking turkey hunting, about which

I knew next to nothing except that you sat still while someone called or scratched on a slate and then you shot the turkey as he strutted in. I was thinking of candied yams, fried okra, sweet potato pie, and perhaps a julep or two on the porch come evening.

I believe it was shortly before 3 A.M. when I was awakened from a sleep troubled by a well-deserved indigestion, and not long after, I found myself, still less than half awake, paddling a canoe in the pitch dark while my guide, who is a surgeon between turkey seasons, was imitating the call of a barred owl. At infrequent intervals we would go ashore and set up our turkey decoy. Then the guide would rummage up a call from the dozen or so he carried and I would peer into the woods while he orchestrated the sweet and plaintive sound of the spinster hen. Now and then he would elbow me and silently mouth "did you hear something?" And I, who can barely hear it thunder, would shake my head in a solemn negative.

In the sovereign state of Virginia, wisdom has scarcely dimin-
ished since the days of Jefferson, Madison, and Monroe. Thoughtful intelligence has even infiltrated the ranks of the fish and game
department, which has decreed that at noon, all turkey hunting
must cease and its participants must have an antacid and a nap.
This I did as swiftly and gratefully as I have ever done anything,
and when I awoke I was ready for come-what-may.

The evening came to focus around a small sportsmen's dinner for
Dr. McCarty and his friends who, when alerted that a Yankee was
loose, were determined that he should not be allowed to waste
away. I do not recall everything—the human mind can only cope
with so much before the circuits overload—but I do recall smoked
turkey, venison, homemade breads, maybe a dozen different vegetables, and roast pork. It seemed that each lady had made three different kinds of pie. I did not sleep well and I did not sleep long.

I was to be spared the canoe the next morning. Instead, I was
introduced to precipice scaling by touch. I was expected not only
not to fall or stun myself witless by walking into a tree, but to do
so with the quiet stealth of a Green Beret. The decoy was again
placed and the calls brought into play. I offered up my body to a
variety of winged and wingless creatures who, while having never
tasted Yankee before, found it quite to their liking. Now and then
the good doctor would poke me and point carefully to a place in
the woods and nod and make the motions of getting ready. I was
ready, but mostly for the hands on my watch to whip swiftly towards noon.

That evening, a new group had their shot at moving my belt to
the last notch, and they enjoyed considerable success. The next
morning we were allowed to sleep in until a few minutes after 3.
Back to the canoe, but this time only briefly for transport. Shortly
before dawn even I could hear the gobbler's loud warning to lesser
males and his promises of undreamed delights to the plastic hen.

I watched him circle around us for a good half hour, scratching and strutting through the leaves and brush, his wings curved in a gesture of might, his head cocked with self esteem, and his brain keeping him just a few yards beyond shooting distance.

Virginia, unlike many states, has always had a turkey season, and I'm told (and I believe it) that their wild turkeys are truly wilder than most. At any rate, this one was, and still is, as far as I know. It was a delightful and exciting experience for me, and now I am close to understanding the passion the turkey can arouse. It has to be a powerful passion to have won the toss between staying in bed or imitating an owl long before dawn.

It was time to start the long drive home. We were tentatively making plans for next year when one hunter, heavy lidded and yawning, agreed that the whole experience had been incredible and worth repeating next season, but could he suggest a different place.

"Where?" someone asked.

"Downtown New Orleans," he answered.

Well, that's certainly down South and it suits me fine. But in the meantime I have already bought an owl hooter and am practicing on it just in case this great idea, like so many others in our history, dies aborning.

○ *A SECRET PLACE*

I NEVER ACTUALLY heard the name of the town. When someone talked about it, they'd say "the river where the church has the trout weathervane," or "the place where they have the organ and the singing fisherman." It is agreed, generally, that there's a good local fly tier and a small boarding house that serves wonderful food—or used to; the stories vary.

The town is supposed to be somewhere along the line where Vermont and New York state touch. I'm really not sure if it's in one state or the other. I've thought, now and then, of taking a little time off and driving around there; but, so far, I haven't been able to find the time. I have no doubt I'd recognize it, although I don't know anyone who has actually been there. I get the impression that the river sits at the bottom of a deep valley and you can't see it until you crest the hills that cup the village, and that the first thing you notice is the church steeple with a huge trout weathervane hammered out of copper by whoever it was that caught the fish.

Years ago, so another story goes, a wealthy fisherman—thought to be English—gave a fine organ to the church and encouraged anyone who could to use it. Apparently they did, and often, so I've heard, when the evening wind is a soft westerly, those fishing in the quieter pools can hear the threads of Bach and Mozart and Handel and the like. "These may be the most lovely evenings on earth," I heard an angler say when some mention was made of the little village; when I asked him where it was, he said he's never actually been there himself, but he often imagined what it would be like.

It was always that way. Someone would mention the place with the wonderful stream and the organ and someone else would say they knew someone who had been there. Others would say they'd read something about it, and almost everyone was sure it had been discovered by Theodore Gordon, who shared it with a few of his friends. There was also talk of a lady who lives there who is a startling beauty and a fisherman with the skill to match any of the greats. It's also said that she had been a famous singer, and at times, when she believes she is alone, you can hear her, but, if she ever sees you, she stops at once. It's believed that the organ players often play some of her favorite melodies when the town is empty of strangers.

The river is thought to produce a number of trout of remarkable size. Theories vary, but it's generally believed that some type of forage fish are there in great numbers and that trout gorge on them; perhaps some shad or alewife. Whatever the reason, it's been pointed out to me that several of the huge trout mounted in this or that club really came from this stream, and that the beautiful lady had taken them and given them to fishermen sworn to secrecy.

Everyone seems pleased to say that the village isn't on any map. A common theory holds that the hard road turns away from the river and the dirt road that runs through it is without a sign. "You have to go with someone who has been there, or you'll never find it" is the most authoritative direction I ever heard. Once when I stopped for supper at an inn in Pennsylvania, in the lounge, an old gentleman asked if he could join me, and took almost an hour telling me what the place was like in the warming days of early spring. "The strangest part of the place at this time of the year is the fragrance of the air. It's sweet, but not cloying—the sort of lingering scent you notice only when a particularly lovely woman passes by; you can't describe it, but the memory of it is always with you. The water, for some reason—probably an odd local mineral deposit—of-

The gentleman on my left is Ed Zern. The many, many days we've spent together have been all too few and all too short.

ten seems to have a slight tint of blue. The way the water ought to be fished, upstream, it seems that the wind always favors a right-handed caster. There's a small path that runs along the stream and behind that an old log road the town fishermen keep cleared, so that you always have room for your backcast." He smiled, as if involved in his favorite memory, and, with half-closed eyes, described a ledge here, a sweeper hemlock there, a particular rock that always shared a trout if the fly was put just so in the current tongue. I could see it as clearly myself, so lovingly was it described. He became quiet for a minute, and as I was about to ask him specific directions, I saw that he'd drifted off to sleep. I left him and when I looked for him later, he'd gone and none of the other guests seemed to know his name—just passing through, they guessed.

It was this sort of thing that had me intrigued—bits and pieces about the little town and its legends kept coming along here and there as the flames ebbed in the fireplaces and dreams danced in the embers. It never seemed to matter that no one really knew much more than the size of the trout and the church and the music. It was generally assumed that sooner or later we'd find ourselves there walking along the bank making untroubled casts, the wind always being in the right direction and the water as blue as a loved one's eyes. In the meantime, we all had more immediate and tangible plans. Our talk was filled with stories and plans about the Gunnison, the Deshutes, the Beaverkill, or the like. The more fortunate would make a big scene over their coming trip to the Spey or the Grimsa or Norway, and the rest of us would show the proper envy.

It had occurred to me that rarely when the old anglers talked about "the place" were they talking to me; I just happened to overhear them. I assumed gradually that all this secrecy and pretense was because the river was part of a private club. I knew that there were still several semi-secret such places that only the members talked about, and then mainly to each other, and that outsiders weren't supposed to know much more than that there were such clubs, until, if and when, they were asked along as a guest. Here was an explanation that I could live with, and I thought less and less about the white church with the trout weathervane lying below me as I topped the hill, although there were times, maybe once or twice a year, that in some lost and lonely place I would find myself completely still, listening, imagining I could hear someone singing and soft chords echoing from nowhere.

On the other hand, I knew that there is always a "secret place" that everyone seems to know a lot about except where it is. Maybe this was just a myth that started, Lord knows where or when, and had just enough thread of possibility that the more imaginative could weave their own dreams into it. It could be the "certain knowledge" of places like the elephants' graveyard that still exists around some African campfires. The cities of gold, the lost mines, the river of diamonds still glow in the imagination of some men awaiting only the breath of the adventurer-dreamer to bring them into warming flames.

I see myself as a rational man. I don't waste much time with daydreams of sudden wealth or glory. I'm generally uncomfortable with grown men believing in what amounts to mere folklore—but the more I think about this secret river, I lean to "Why not?" Perhaps, someday, I'll look up from a river I've never fished before, and see a copper trout swinging in the wind and hear some Lorelei challenging me to find her in a place I can't see, but know is not too far away. There are worse things to think about than saving the best for last.

A really fine sable from Zambia, made even more memorable by listening to the lions at 3 A.M. the next morning quarreling over the carcass just a few feet from my very wakeful eyes.

○ *WE DIDN'T SHOOT*
AN ELEPHANT

I WAS LOOKING at a pair of secretary birds sitting in the top of a thorn tree. It was dusk, and the last light cast a purple tint against the tree, the birds, and the mountains in the distance. I remember thinking that, like a lot of things you see in Africa, it was almost too beautiful to be real; it was as if you had been wishing for something but didn't know what, and suddenly there it was.

On the side of the mountain, way back in the fading light, in an odd relief as if they were part of some bizarre puzzle of tree and birds, I saw the elephants.

The three bulls were just *there*, that magical way elephants often appear in Africa. In a minute they were gone so completely you wondered if you had really seen them. But our hunter, Dave Ommanney, had seen them too. "The best ivory I've seen in years," "Close to 90 pounds—and I know where they'll be tomorrow."

At the start I had no intention of shooting an elephant. None of us did. Good elephants in Kenya were rare, as always, and my mind couldn't encompass the idea of killing one anyway. We'd seen elephants off and on as we drove around, mostly small bulls and cows. One lone patriarch safely tucked behind the borders of Tsavo National Park had so dwarfed everything else we'd seen that we parked our truck and stared at him for an hour. All of this confirmed the fact that I was not ready to kill an elephant. But Jim Rikhoff, who was on his fourth safari, was eager to do so. I would be an observer. I would hunt the elephant secondhand.

Long before dawn, we were perched on a rocky escarpment over-looking a valley where we were sure the elephants would appear. And indeed they did; but not our elephants. Every so often we would discover, through our glasses, a group of cows and small bulls. It was eerie how they came in and out of our sight—like suddenly seeing a gas station where none had been a minute before. But none of them had the long, heavy ivory that we had seen in our restive sleep the night before.

"They've possibly gone back into the park," David said. "But maybe not. I want to go one more day."

I remember it being about mid-morning when one of the trackers we had posted in the top of a tall tree came back and said he had seen elephants coming. David smiled. Jim lit the wrong end of a cigarette. As far as I could see there was nothing I could climb in case I had to. David checked his .375. I checked my shoelaces.

In general, the cover was big brush, the kind of brush you wouldn't want to gun quail or woodcock in because it was too thick. That was only one of the reasons I didn't think this was the sort of adventure that Selous or Bell would have lept into, let alone Hill and Rikhoff, who were already famous for doing things that are better left to the imagination. I fell a little further behind Ommanney, who was herding Jim in front of him like a goat.

And suddenly there they were, or at least their tops—tops of spines, tops of heads, tops of ears. Later David said 40 yards, but I still doubt it was that far. We stood there unable to see ivory, unable to see anything except the tip of an ear and a patch of hide as they moved slowly around in front of us.

The word "impasse" struck me as perfect. David and Jim were crouched like stone dogs on a lawn. The tracker, who had gone up his tree again, now came down, crept up to David, and motioned him to come back. David tugged Jim's belt and they walked backwards out of the thicket until they came to the little clearing where I waited. David whispered that they were cows with calves, and we had best walk away and do it quickly and quietly.

Back at the truck, David told us that the bulls must have gone into the park and it would be a waste of time to wait on the chance they might return, so we'd best go look for our lesser kudu. Neither Jim nor I argued. We had been close to the truth with the cow elephants, and the answers we found to the questions we all ask ourselves weren't too bad.

I've been on several safaris since our day with the elephants, and I've taken some very fine heads and had some exciting moments to think about. But I keep seeing that mountain in Kenya, the three bulls there washed purple in the near dark. I think it is the one thing I will always remember about Africa.

Not far from where we saw the elephants, I understand there is now a hotel for tourists. And I sometimes wonder if our three bulls ever stand off in the darkness and listen to the music coming from the hotel; the way I once stood and listened to the calling of shrikes. Somehow I have a picture of these three old gentlemen smiling to themselves, lost in wonder at the strange things going on, missing the peace and quiet you need when you're old and want to call up better times.

Often when Jim and I are together now, one of us will say, "Remember the elephants?" And then we'll both be silent for a bit while we think about Kenya, and remember the romance, the adventure, and the insolence of being young.

Neither of us has ever said that we're glad we didn't shoot an elephant. We don't have to.

Rough shooting on the Isle of Lewis off the coast of Scotland. The gun is a Henry Atkin, the birds are red grouse and the costume is both functional and comfortable.

○ *ADVENTURES*

FROM TIME TO TIME, I like to look through my old scrapbook at mementoes from places where I've enjoyed my little adventures. When I do, I am reminded of how many trips I almost didn't take, and I realize that the older I get, the easier it is to talk myself into saying "yes" whenever I feel a need to lose part of myself in the trails on the mountainsides and the paths along rivers. I don't regret spending a little too close to the bone because everything seems to work out in the end, and the worries are more often of my own making than real.

An adventure doesn't have to be centered around the remote or the exotic; an adventure is essentially a frame of mind, an escape from our everyday 9 to 5 worries or problems we can really cope with: Should we wade out far enough to risk getting a dunking? Should we stay with this track and risk coming back after dark?

One memorable adventure took me to a northern Quebec river that was, at the time, literally an "undiscovered" Atlantic salmon river. It had been fished only by Inuit who were hunting caribou in the area for their winter meat. No doubt some white trappers and north country wanderers had been lured by pools teeming with brook trout and salmon in the late summer, but I was probably the first sport to fish it with a fly.

It was a lovely river to walk, and I was compelled to wander the banks, curve after curve, because there is a certain magic to a river's bending that forces you to turn with it—just *because*. Here and there were stone circles marking the camping places of Indians who had come and gone in their own migrations two hundred miles or so from the land they called home along the edge of the sea. As I had walked in their tracks, looking for likely spots to fish, so a mother black bear and her cub walked in mine as I discovered later; now and then a small band of caribou would churn through the water I was fishing, their urgency to be somewhere else overcoming any fear of me.

At night when it was dark enough, I would stand outside to see the northern lights. I was as mystified as an ancient savage at their eerie splendor and felt as if I ought to pray to some northern god and thank him for letting me be here, far from ordinary things.

An outing is something more than a normal hunting or fishing outing, but an outing can turn into an adventure. To me, an adventure is a happening that alters the mind, involves us in a basic, elemental way by stirring up some ancient blood, and shows us a side of ourselves that we might have forgotten. An outing might make us laugh at ourselves, or expose a weakness or vanity; but an adventure ought to involve a decision out of the ordinary and throw some light on one of our dark sides.

I've had adventures that were frightening and adventures that were funny. I've been out on big water in a small boat when the weather suddenly turned the color gray that I normally associate with graveyards and pall bearers. And I've shoved a canoe out in a river with all the *elan* of either Lewis or Clark and then noticed that both my paddles were right where I'd left them—back on shore.

The good thing about adventures is that they mostly just happen, hopefully when you need one to stir up your life. But you have to be there. You have to get up and go; you have to try to live your life so you can sit back in years to come and say "I remember when . . . " instead of "I should have . . . " It's not easy, but then nothing worthwhile is.

I doubt if I've ever been much happier than when messing around in Africa. Not a world class rifleman, I probably have successfully relied on my .375 again to bail me out.

A lot of my own adventures have been exercises of the mind. When we are in the country of great bears, we can justify imagining them lurking nearby in the dark—even if we don't really see any. It's the idea, the possibility that adds spice to the high country, or running the rapids, wading around in a duck marsh full of pot-holes—*something* is waiting there to happen.

This year when something that might be especially interesting comes along, I'm going to take a long walk while I make up my mind. I'm going to check my personal ledger and see how long it's been since I've seen the great mountains, fished a river new to me, been in the company of good bird dogs, got caught in a soaking rain, or been snowed in, thoroughly confused, or plain and honest lost. When was the last time I hit it just exactly right? And since the answer to that is close to "never," I have to believe, as I always do, that this may be the trip.

We need to exercise the mind, the imagination, and the spirit as well as the body. We owe ourselves the quickening of the secret pulses when we know that something unknown might lie ahead. What a pitiful world it would be without the possibility, real or not, of something bizarre swimming in the depths or lurking in an undiscovered cave.

I've been lucky enough to have smelled the breath of elephants and heard lions crunching bones. I've run some whitewater with my eyes closed in willful ignorance, trusting to *something* to see me through. I've been in places and situations where I didn't dare look down and at times where I didn't dare look up—the stuff and the heart of adventure.

Adventures live forever—coming back whenever you need something to brighten an otherwise empty day, or to push you into saying "yes" to the promise of another. An adventure anywhere is something you can save, a little magic you can always call on and take with you when you close the kitchen door and take a walk with the dog in the dark.

○ *GOOD ENOUGH*

WHILE POKING through some old books and magazines I came across a "letter to my grandson" piece I'd written a long while back. I'd bet that any grandson of mine or yours won't be surprised by the antics of the world he's growing up in. But I know how surprised my grandfather would be if he were to come back for a couple of days and take a look around.

I'd start him off with the fact that the trendy drink is bottled water with a twist of lemon peel, about $2-plus a serving. Give him the hard news first. Now about paying close to $15 for a box of high brass duck loads? Would he believe that his $75 VH Parker is worth (or at least sells for) about what he once paid for a new Model T Ford?

My grandfather, who was overly fond of sayings he remembered from some almanac, used to lecture me about how important it was to be in the right place at the right time. I don't know what place he's in right now, but I do know he got there at the right time.

How would Grandfather feel about running steel shot through his duck gun? Or hearing a bass fisherman shout "cross that hawg's eyes!" I know he wouldn't understand how the cost of a hunting license could have gone up close to fifty times, and that hunting—well, let's say it isn't quite the same.

He used to like a quiet evening on the lake casting an old plug to the edge of the lily pads. He rowed out there quietly, fished quietly, talked quietly. He wasn't a church-going man but he often sang hymns quietly to himself—"The Old Rugged Cross," "The Little Brown Church," "Rock of Ages." If he spoke at all on those rare occasions when I had a bass on instead of a lily pad, he'd say, "Isn't that wonderful!" And it was just as wonderful if the bass got away. He taught me, softly, the difference between fishing and trying to catch fish.

Grandfather would not be completely surprised at the changes in our trapping laws. He was a trapper and a fur trader, a buyer and seller. He believed that I would learn more about "woodcraft"

running my small trapline than any other way. I agreed with him, and still do. We were farmers then, men and women who were involved in birth and death and all its beautiful and dreadful mutations, and we didn't devote much time to abstract concerns.

It would please Grandpa to know that the liberation of our fishing season means the season is rarely closed. He usually fished whenever he could anyway, so I don't know whether he was a poacher or a pioneer.

A deer was a wonder to Grandpa, as much because of its grace and magic as its scarcity, and he would enjoy the burgeoning of our deer herd. I used to think it odd that he found reasons to keep from joining the other men during deer season. And when he did go, I don't remember him bringing home any venison. He was never considered a good shot and often joked about it himself. Perhaps he sang hymns in the woods as well as on the lake—I like to think he did.

In our current spate of letters to grandsons, the legator leaves the stripling his Garrison rod, his Parker shotgun, and maybe a secret map of the best bird covers in the state. My grandfather never knew who Garrison or his ilk were, nor did he care. His fishing tackle, some of which I still have, was part homemade, part stuff left in the boats he rented out during the summer. He had some old, cheap spoons and plugs, and his bass rod and reel were nothing to covet, even by a small farmboy.

"Good enough" was a phrase that came very easily to Grandfather in matters of appraisal. (Where I was concerned, "good enough" was even more flexible.) His shotgun was cheap but sound, like his ax and his other tools. I suspect he had the Methodist's disdain for pride in worldly goods; other than his horses and sleighs, the auction after his funeral was little more than a parceling of the same indifferent stuff every farmer had in plenty. It seems to me that the old farmers then took what little pride they allowed themselves in skills, not tools. My grandfather would be shocked to see how much things have become back-end-to.

Grandfather would be surprised to see us living with so many restrictions. I doubt if he ever saw a NO TRESPASSING sign. He wouldn't understand the urge for noise and speed in a fishing boat, or why he couldn't buy a "good enough" casting reel for $10 or $15. He wouldn't have liked electronic fish finders or bottom scanners; he enjoyed the mystery of fishing, the thought of a 10-pound bass lying sullenly in an unfathomable hole.

I know Grandfather would have been opposed to wearing "hunter orange" as well as to laws that would have prevented him from taking his seven-year-old grandson in the woods with his own gun. Grandfather would have loved camouflage.

Modern coolers and bass lures that rattled would have appealed to Grandfather; he was forever attached to an old Pflueger plug because it "glowed in the dark." He would have liked boats that didn't need painting and caulking so often. And one pair of "good enough" binoculars, since he was always looking for something.

If I could bring Grandfather back for one more evening of fishing together, I know what would be "good enough" to make him smile all over—one of those personal battery tape players with Willie Nelson and Tom T. Hall, and Waylon and Dolly, and a few by some good gospel singers. I can see him now, rolling his head back to take in the infinite night above and softly joining in the singing while his dimly glowing Pflueger plug frightened the bass into immobility.

○ *WHEN NO ONE IS LOOKING*

IT WAS NEARLY a two-hour walk to the woodcock cover that I favored, not a major expedition when you're fourteen, but still, two hours is two hours. I'd been looking forward all week to this Saturday; according to the old-timers, everything was perfect—a full moon, a northeast wind, and mild nights. If the birds were ever going to be down, it was right now. The last turn in the dirt road that bordered the long, winding popple stand always held a certain magic for me; on the left side were the popples and on the right, just a couple of feet higher and drier, were the birches. I always hunted the popples first because the birds I flushed or shot at and missed would almost always swing across the road and into the birches, where it was a lot more open. Figuring this out gave me a highly exaggerated idea of my bird sense that I cherished for years. I guess I was on a level of intelligence with a three-month-old setter puppy. I have gotten somewhat smarter.

Just before I turned the corner where my hunting would begin, I was cheerily greeted by a handsome tricolor setter, tinkling a small bell on his collar. I had known his owner for years, but my heart fell as I realized Judge Landis either was about to enter my cover or had just finished hunting it. He must have seen me first, because he was leaning up against his yellow Packard and holding an apple in his hand. He tossed it over and I put it in my pocket.

The Judge as often as not hunted wearing his business suit, over which he'd pull a pair of farmer's bib overalls. I don't ever remember seeing him without a necktie. The little door on the side of the convertible was open—it was called a golf-club compartment—and I could see the leather shotgun cases.

"Good morning, sir," I said.

"And good morning to you," he replied with a smile. He was one of my hunting heroes and I suspect he knew it. "I gather you are a fancier of *Philohela minor*," he said, "and you have been listening to all that nonsense from the loafers at the post office about the full

The thin one is the painter, Dave Maass. He's a very close friend and other than that I can think of no other reason to be in Minnesota in winter.

moon and you are standing there wondering if I've left you any birds, right?"

"Yes, sir," I said, trying to keep Rufus from licking my face any more.

"How often have you hunted this cover?"

"Twice last year," I replied. "My father and I found some birds in it last fall when we were looking for a place to set mink traps."

"Did you get any mink?"

"Two, sir."

"Did you get any birds?"

"Three the first time, and only one the next."

"How many shells?" he asked, looking at my single-barrel 20-gauge.

"Almost half a box," I answered.

"These things take time, of course, and I notice that you aren't hunting with a dog. Rufus is a marvel on woodcock."

"So I've heard," I said.

"May I make a suggestion?" the Judge said after a pause.

"Yes sir," and I knew what he was going to say and it was like a dream come true. I'm sure I was smiling as hard as I was trying not to.

"If you would be so kind as to do me two favors, I would greatly appreciate it."

"What are they, sir?" I asked him.

"Well, here I am with a new 16-gauge from England, a company by the name of Boss, and I can't wait to use it. On the other hand, I want to give Rufus a good workout since I'm sure we're going to be into birds, and I'll need some help. Would you mind using my old 20-gauge Parker? I think the two guns are an advantage over one, and between us I believe we could do justice to Rufus. We could sort of back each other up if we have to; hate to see a dog work hard and not have the reward of a retrieve. What do you say?"

I handed him my single-barrel, carefully opened, and he slid it into the golfclub compartment after he withdrew the two leather cases. I will remember the look and smell of the Boss as long as I live, and the fear that I would fall and scratch the Parker he'd put together and handed me. He made no condescending chatter about gun safety, merely said that the gun had an automatic safety and was bored pretty open in both barrels.

The Judge noticed that I was walking a little gingerly into the alders, and he took a minute to point out that the gun was his bird gun, already had plenty of "good honest scratches," and one or two more wouldn't hurt any.

Rufus was as good as I'd heard, and the loafers down at the post office were right, for once. The flight was in and the morning was such that I still, all these years later, sometimes wonder if I'd only imagined this or if it really happened. After I'd gone through my six or eight shells, the Judge put a couple of handfuls in my pockets and told me not to be nervous. We often shot side by side over a point, and the Judge claimed that most of his shooting was just insurance and that I may have been born just so I could handle his Parker. I think this was the first of many, but not enough, days when shooting had the magical aspect of being "perfect." I had never gunned with a person like the Judge—in truth, I had hardly gunned with anyone at all other than my father—I had never seen a bird dog like Rufus, nor had I ever before been into birds seemingly spaced the ideal time apart. I dreaded the moment when the Judge would pull out his pocket watch and then close the cover down on the day of days.

Close to noon the Judge called in Rufus and snapped the leash on his collar, opened his gun and left it open across his arm. I did the same with the Parker and handed him the two shells that had been in it. They were the last of the handfuls he had given me. "Better keep those," he said. "I don't believe there's a more empty feeling than having a gun over your arm and not a single shell in your pocket."

On the walk back to the car the Judge chatted about this and that—just as if I were a grownup friend of his—and something inside me changed; I could almost hear a *click*, the sort of sound the hour hand makes on a grandfather clock. A couple of hours ago I was just an ordinary boy; now I was something else. I wasn't sure what I was but I was something else—I was *thinking* differently than I ever had. I suddenly knew that someday I would be somebody like the Judge, that I would have my own Parker and my own Rufus, my own Packard—I could see it all happening, and I wasn't afraid of it as I had been before. It was like I was walking alongside

someone I used to know; it was a little scary but in a nice way, like seeing your reflection all broken up in the ripples of a lake.

At the car we watered Rufus, and the Judge put the guns up and slid them back into the little compartment, "I've got the time to drop you off close to home, if you'd like," he said. I said I'd like that very much, if it wasn't too much trouble. "No trouble at all," he said, tugging the bill of my corduroy cap down over my eyes a little, the way men will do. "We're friends, hunting partners, how could it be too much trouble?"

I tried to tell him how I felt, how much I'd enjoyed his allowing me to go along, but words didn't come easily to me then. He said he understood and that the pleasure was all his and he thanked me for helping him work Rufus. Then he asked me a strange question. He said, "What does hunting mean to you, besides shooting something to give to your mother for the table?"

I couldn't begin to sort out all the things that were in my head—I don't think I've got them all sorted out yet—but he really didn't want to hear what I had to say; he just wanted to answer his own question. He wasn't being rude; it was simply part of his manner.

"I think a lot about hunting; it's a complicated piece of business," he said. "But I remember one thing that came to me when I was a little older than you are, I was out by myself, with one of my father's good bird dogs—and one of his good guns. He didn't mind; he believed that things are meant to be used. And while I was out, I had what I like to think of as a T-H-O-U-G-H-T." (He spelled it out and it sounded like it was all in capital letters.) "I haven't had all that many, so they're not all that hard to remember. I was hunting grouse, and a young bird flew up in front of the dog and landed on a branch of some kind of pine . . . tamarack, maybe. I had already missed three or four and hated to come home empty-handed; my father always had something to say about *that*. I swung the gun up on that bird, and then I put it down. That's when I had my THOUGHT: I thought that here I was alone, doing the right thing—a thing I knew that many men wouldn't blink an eye over—and that I was in the most vulnerable of moments—*when no one is looking*. I knew then that I'd turn out all right. I knew then that I was an honest person. *That I could trust myself.* What do you think of that?"

I thought about it without saying anything. The Judge didn't really want an answer as much as he wanted an audience. He went on about law being the civilizing structure and was quoting himself when we came up to the lane that led to our farm. He stopped the car and got out and walked a few steps with me while he told me that it had been his pleasure to have had my company, and some other things like that. No one had ever talked to me tht way before in my life, and as a matter of fact it was a good many years before I met another man with the natural good manners of the Judge. We shook hands, made an indefinite date to meet, and he promised that if he could, he'd drop by the farm on his way gunning to see if I might be free.

I began thinking about the Judge trusting himself, sometimes in the context of hunting but more often not. It got to be a joke between me and the Judge in later years. We did meet gunning every so often, and true to his word he stopped by the farm now and then to see if I could go. My father respected him very much and would gladly take on some of my work in order for me to spend a little time with what he called an "educated person."

I was on vacation from college and, feeling homesick to chat about dogs and shotguns, I went to the Judge's home. A maid answered the door, and before she could even ask me to wait, the Judge had come out from a room on the hall and was shoving me into his study. The maid brought us tea and he asked about college and I asked about the bird covers and how Rufus II was coming along. I reminded him of the day we first gunned together and the story he told me about discovering that he was an honest man.

"I think I am, too," I said. "I'm not as sure as I think you were, but I'm pretty sure."

"I think I shall ask my wife to refer to me, in private of course, as Diogenes," he said.

We both smiled and I said goodby.

We continued to see each other, not often of course, but enough so that "Diogenes" became another private joke between us—not a funny joke, really, but more a term of understanding, a basis of rank in a philosophical way.

During my last Thanksgiving vacation, I'd come home and gone to see him. He wasn't feeling well and asked me to do him a favor. "Of course," I said.

"Old Rufus the Deuce has been driving me crazy. Would you take one of the shotguns and stick him in the woods for an hour or so?"

I said I'd go right now if that was all right with him. I piled into the car and Rufus calmed down and went to sleep on the back seat. We drove back to a corner much like the one where years before I'd met the Judge, and I found a likely-looking cover and turned Rufus out while I put the old Parker together. A lot of things had changed, but one thing was as constant as truth and that was the sound of the fore-end clicking into place and the lock closing on the barrels. I opened the gun up and closed it again, with my eyes shut, just to hear the faint *ting* the barrels made.

I looked at the gun I held and at Rufus II watching me with his cataract-heavy eyes. I can still remember how pure was the wave of happiness I felt standing there—where no one was looking—and saying, out loud to a young man who wouldn't ever be there again, "I gather you are a fancier of *Philohela minor*." And then, so I wouldn't forget it, I started to tell Rufus II the story of how I first met the Judge—because I like the sound and the import of the words, especially when he got to the part about a T-H-O-U-G-H-T and knowing he was an honest person.

○ *WHAT IF?*

D R E A M E R S   A R E   always dreaming about some perfect place—
the kind of spot where the grass might be greener. You could call
it the "what if?" condition.

When I'm deer hunting, I'm always shifting, however slightly,
from one good stand to another. Fishing is even worse; the best
spot always seems to be across the river, or where someone else is
already staked out. If I'm fortunate enough to be in Stuttgart up
to my wader tops in big greenheads, I'll likely be dreaming about
being in my favorite waterblind in Maryland.

Of course the question "What if?" has no basis in reality. I know,
because I've tested it. I've made people change places with me
along the river and I never seem to catch more fish. Last fall I was
lucky enough to be in Mexico with a large number of 28-gauge
shells and a steady stream of whitewing doves coming in. My
shooting, with a borrowed gun, was not outstanding. The man next
to me was bringing down impossibly high incomers, centering
downwind right angles, etc., etc. There was no question in my mind
that his gun was better than mine, so at lunch time I managed to
wheedle, or shame, or bore him into trading off with me. Predictably, he shot as he had in the morning and so, predictably, did I.

As a once-dedicated trapshooter, I have become permanently
convinced that someone, somewhere, has a gun that is the answer
to all my problems. The two of us will probably never meet. Chances are good that the same man will have a 28-inch side-by-side that

*Typically unprepared for where I was
hunting I had the good luck to be
with Jay Herbert whose back, I hear,
is much, much better now.*

would inspire me to the latent greatness I know is there—I wouldn't object at all if it was a hammer gun.

Being in the wrong place at the wrong time is a universal problem. It may be unrealistic to believe that *everyone* is always in this fix, but it seems that many a hunter and fisherman is so afflicted.

I called a friend in Michigan recently to brag a little about how well I'd done on Pennsylvania mourning doves. Hoping he'd had a three-day rain, or the cycle was on the down side, or his shooting was off, or his dog was as wild as mine usually are, I asked him how he'd done on the early grouse and woodcock. The second he said, "Sensational . . . ," I was tempted to hang up. He kept hitting me where it hurt by saying, over and over, "You should have been there!" Of course I should have been there, but if I had been there, it would have rained, the cycle would have been down, and I would have brought the wrong gun. And would they have had a weekend with the doves in Pennsy!

What's worse is when you're there, in the wrong place and fully exposed, for everyone to see. For example, you're dove shooting and all the birds are pouring toward the tree you're sitting under. To someone who doesn't know dove shooting, this would seem like the perfect place to be. Wrong! The experienced dove shooter knows that too much action tends to short circuit the nervous system, especially when the birds are high incomers. There are eight common places to point the gun at a fast, right-at-you dove, and only one is the right one. You will continue to shoot behind or off to one side of every bird that centers on you, and even the most senile of witnesses will remember your performance to his last breath. The right place to be at a dove shoot is where all, or most, of your birds are the easy right-to-left crossing shots—the kind the guy sitting next to you always has.

The easy-looking prone shot in open antelope country can also be the wrong place. To the group watching me in such a situation in Wyoming, it seemed a foregone conclusion that I had my tag filled when I stretched out behind my .257 Roberts. *They* didn't see that imperceptible knoll; all I could see was grass and sod. When I moved to try a sitting position, the antelope got spooky and sort of crouched just as I shot. That's *really* why I missed.

"What if . . . ?" Sometimes it's better that we don't know. It can be more pleasant to imagine what tomorrow might bring than to know for certain. Tomorrow just might be the day when it all comes together in the bird field, even for that young Missy dog. Tomorrow our casts could be long and straight, the fly cocked as perfectly as you'd wish.

Outdoorsmen are odd creatures. We're restless. Most of our forefathers crossed an ocean and a continent chasing their dreams or ideals—and not a few just for the hell of it. When we get to thinking, we realize there's so much going on that we'll never get to most of it, or even what we feel should be our little share. It tends to nag at us.

I could be in the right blind on the right day, with the right shotgun, or in the river surrounded by rising trout savaging my fly. And suddenly here it comes. What if I had 8's in both barrels instead of 6's? Suppose I went out and moved those goose decoys a little more off to the left? What if I changed to an Adams in a little smaller size?

Someone who doesn't understand might say we're not very bright; others could appreciate our curiosity and our questing spirit. The truth is, we're pulled by a strange force, the way the moon tugs at the sea. "What if . . . ?"

○ HUNTING DEER

I SHOT MY FIRST deer when I was eleven years old and my final one several times in the past few years. How often have I said to myself, "This is my last time?" I've lost count. But just recently I managed to "need" and buy a new .257 Roberts, just for deer hunting.

What changed my mind? The almost incredible number of deer in most parts of the country is one reason. Another is I found I was missing something I needed by not going out, by not being alone on a hunt, by not practicing my woodsmanship. I really don't *need* to take a deer, but I do *need* to be out there in hunting season.

When I was a boy, my otherwise idle mind was occupied with visions of Shawnees and Delawares. Reading about wilderness adventures, I had an overwhelming belief that I was one with the likes of Carson and Boone. I wasted a lot of my time in what might charitably be called sneaking up—or what I thought was sneaking up. I felt almost magic, standing in the woods and seeing a deer that hadn't seen me. I would check the wind like the "Indian" I felt I was and begin my stalk.

I secretly felt, for years longer than made any sense, that I was pretty good at it, until I faced up to the fact that the occasional deer I took was almost never the one I started out after, but instead one someone else had accidentally pushed my way. Still, even more than ever before, I believe that this is the "right" way to hunt deer, especially with our modern rifles and sights, and, even more importantly, in terms of personal satisfaction.

I pleasure in the hours spent studying crossings and scrapes, guessing at wind eddies, the watching and quiet walking, the magic in solving the mystery of *this is what I'd do if I were that deer* and having it come out just that way. No matter if it doesn't; it's a game that I can't lose.

Like most of us, I'm not really hunting a deer as much as pursuing a role, a "pretend" adventure that goes back to the boy I once was. I can't see the clumsy, tow-headed, overdressed, over-mothered boy I once was, but I can see the Shawnee I once was, and I still smile at the memory. I am hunting *him* when he was hunting deer. There are millions of us doing the same thing every season.

Every deer camp is filled with kids of all ages, kids burning their once-a-year attempts at pancakes, wrenching their backs splitting stove wood, staying up past their bedtime playing cards, wearing their hats and red suspenders at the table, and sleeping in their underwear, the same underwear, for days at a time. These are kids with rifles and sheath knives and thick plaid shirts, and new (and hopefully) waterproof boots, compasses and packs full of self-made, half-pound sandwiches and heart-warming concoctions in vacuum flasks. This is camping out at its very, very best!

No doubt much of the appeal of hunting deer is the chance—the one chance most of us have—to really get away. It's a chance to work our way back into the tall timber, to be a moving hunter, a planner, a solver of problems. It's a chance to meld instinct with knowledge, to think about woodcraft, to move in search of an animal that is the most challenging trophy of all. If you want to have a hard hunt, if you want something very special sticking to your own levels of accomplishment, the whitetail buck is the one you dream about.

I like the idea of a hunter saying to himself, "Ten-pointer or nothing." I respect him. I know he'll have worked hard, and win or lose, he'll be satisfied that his way is the right one. But sometimes I just want to hunt, and I'll pretty much take what comes along. On a ranch I sometimes hunt I let the eight- and ten-pointers go by and I work on the spikes; the rancher wants somebody to cull, and I'm perfectly satisfied to do it. When I hunt there, my mind is on backstraps and inch-thick chops and fresh liver.

I like to walk the bottoms and listen to the wild turkeys, hoping to see a bobcat as much as I'm hoping not to see a rattler. I like sitting still, listening to the cardinals and watching a shadow, hoping it will be something magic, like the otters I watched for hours in a dark place in Alabama or the hunting owl in Pennsylvania.

I doubt if ever there was or ever will be any more passionate pursuer of game than the American deer hunter. Pick your kind of country—farmland, swamp, high timber, desert mountains—you name it and you can find deer in it. You can stalk, sit, drive, climb a tree, even run hounds in some states. You can be skillful or you can be lucky; it probably won't make much difference. I suspect

that just as many deer are stumbled over, in a way, as are taken with stealth and marksmanship. No matter what or who you are, you've got a chance to hang your venison on the pole.

When I killed my first deer, at age eleven, I got my picture on the front page of the local weekly paper. Deer were scarce, times were hard, and even a little good news about a kid's first deer was worth writing about. Today, not far from where I was brought up, my little farm is grazed and browsed to within an inch of disaster by deer. It's a virtual 100 percent bet that any evening at dusk I can show you half a dozen or more whitetails in my fields.

Deer have eaten or scraped my favorite trees. They've made us move our garden to the middle of the backyard, and at night I don't drive my lane much faster than I can walk. But the sight of "my" triplet fawns pawing the fallen apples is still wild and haltingly lovely, and something always makes me stop and watch in admiration when one of the bucks takes center stage in the meadow.

It's been a couple of years since I've shot a deer now, although I've had my chances. The buck was either too young and sprightly, or so old he had my sympathetic understanding. There might have been a sapling in the way or maybe he was just too far away.

You know just how it can happen—the boy says *shoot* and the man says *wait,* and while you discuss this deep inside, the deer has moved away. The boy says, he'll be back next season, and the man, thinking of many dark things, says, *I hope so.*

○ *A LOVE LETTER*

DEAR JOE:

I'm delighted you and your new puppy are getting along so well. I know it's been a long time since you've had a brand-new dog, and I know this is your first Labrador, so I thought I'd take a few minutes to tell you some things about Labs that you might not know.

I'm sure your life has already been drastically altered. First off, you've discovered that Lab pups love to worry the lamp cords. This is not just because lamp cords are in neat places—like behind chairs and sofas where you can't see the pup until you hear the crash—but because, in my opinion, Labs like a house a little on the dark side. They think it's good for you to stumble around in the dark; it's fine training for those early morning walks out to the duck blind when you've forgotten your flashlight like the rest of us always do.

I hope you haven't made the same mistake I did with Maggie—going out with her while she went to the bathroom. She got so she wouldn't do any business unless I was standing there. No matter if it was raining—she likes standing in the rain—or if it was bitter cold, I had to be there or nothing happened. And, I don't remember her being in too much of a hurry most of the time. I finally broke her out of this habit, but it took about a year and several bad colds, not to mention some suspicious looks from my neighbors when they saw me lurking around the yard after dark. I know how you feel and how we all worry, but the only right way is to let the dog out by itself—right from the start.

You ought to get a yardstick from the paint store. I find it's the best thing for putting tennis balls, leather bones, squeaky toys, etc., back into play after they've gotten under the stove, behind the refrigerator, and the thousand other places you don't think about until you are babysitting a puppy. Brooms and mops won't work because the puppy thinks they are part of the game and they will continue to play with them even when you're not around. An eight-week-old dog can go through a broom or mop in less than 5 minutes. It goes on and on.

I doubt you'll be able to resist buying toys. I never could. But don't buy toys that make a lot of noise, like those with little bells in them. Look for *soft* toys, quiet toys—toys which will allow you to sleep, because the puppy's hours are going to be a little different than yours. I don't know how you react to a bell ringing under the bed at 2 A.M., but I react badly. Actually, you'd better get two yardsticks and keep one upstairs for getting the pup from under the bed. I know your wife said the dog wasn't allowed in the bedroom, but I also know Lab puppies and their owners too well. I'll bet I know who it was that brought the dog upstairs so she wouldn't have to worry about it during the night in case it started to cry or something. Just be real smart for once and don't bring the subject up. New shoes are cheaper than an expensive dinner at which the first courses you have to eat are the silly words you said about who brought the dog upstairs in the first place. One of you will bring the dog upstairs—it doesn't much matter who.

I could remind you to store the good chairs, sofas, and rugs for a while, but it's probably too late. You've seen my house. As I write this, I'm looking at three little throw rugs that are hiding holes in the carpet. The carpet was ruined by Maggie's mother and grandmother, so it doesn't matter a whole lot, but I just bring this up because one of the holes is new and Maggie is almost five years of age. You have to tell it like it is . . .

The dog-hair problem is one reason I've always had black Labs and worn dark suits. Black hair does show up more in ice cubes than yellow Lab hair, but you kind of get used to it. There will be times when you'll swear that a 60-pound Lab has 50 pounds of hair, but you learn to live with that. Certain overly fastidious visitors won't drop by very often. Naturally, there will be Lab hairs all over every pillow in the house. I used to worry about breathing hair down into my lungs, but somehow it doesn't happen.

In spite of sleeping for what seems to be twenty hours a day, all Labs are intrinsically restless. Parts of their world need constant rearranging. Holes will be dug in the lawn and flowerbeds. Tree limbs and huge sticks will be carted from place to place. In time, there will be basic order—a favorite outside place to sleep according to the time of day, a special place in the kitchen and bedroom.

When they aren't sleeping, Labs love games that are a little wild and noisy. Maggie is especially fond of volleyball. But she loves, equally, or perhaps a little more, the half-mile walk up to the mailbox and back. She likes to inspect the driveway drains and the edges of the brook. Sometimes she just stares out into the middle distance over the fields with a visible sense of satisfaction and well-being, rather like a prosperous farmer.

Puppies do the same thing in miniature, but they tend to be easily bored, something you ought to remember when you start training yours. One of the best dogs I ever had would train until she was satisfied with whatever we were doing. Then she would walk off and lay down somewhere and no amount of shouting or threatening could move her. She was a jewel in the field and a fine trial dog as you will remember, but her attitude was often self-indulgent, as if she believed I trained just because I liked to train. There would come a point where she refused to be "used." That used to upset me terribly. But looking back, I suppose I was boring her and wasn't bright enough to notice when she was losing interest.

It's been a while since I had a Lab pup of my own, and I envy you the little things that I'm just now remembering. How wonderfully special their smell is, like a wildflower. I like how a Lab lies on his back, with his belly as taut as a drumhead, his head off to one side as if to say there is nothing in the world as wonderful as me. You'll find that one day your pup will start following you, asking what he can do to help: can he get you something, perhaps, or do you need a sympathetic listener?

You will feel that incredible sense of safety knowing that your small dog is guarding you—from anything and everything that might even hint of unhappiness. I used to feel terribly responsible until I realized my dog was really responsible, totally and forever. She hardly ever lived a moment when I wasn't first in her thinking—from the slightest sound at night that would make her suddenly stand alertly between me and the darkness, to a mid-morning suggestion that I might feel a lot better if she took us out to play.

I remember listening for a scratch at the door or a thump of her tail showing she was glad I was around. I also remember her tiny cold nose probing around the pillow to find out if I had heard the geese coming into the pond with the first light of morning and shouldn't we get up and go see them.

But right now I seem to have forgotten about how she chewed up my best hunting boots and the good belt I carelessly dropped on the floor. I think I'd feel very comfortable sitting on a station wagon seat that was sewn back together with some nylon leader. I don't think I ever saw more clearly than when my eyes were slightly misty watching a small black dog figuring out how to bring me back a foot-long stick through a 4-inch gap in a picket fence.

Right now I'm immensely happy for you, and feeling a little sorry for myself. I think Maggie had better take me out for our evening walk.

> Sneak him a little
> food from the table
> in my name . . .
> Gene

Dave Maass has just shown me how easy it is to paint and made me promise I'd never tell anyone else and I haven't. I did the same thing with him about writing.

○ THE ANNUAL REPORT II

As the speaker shuffles through his notes, a tall, blonde lady steps beside him and removes what might be a pouch of chewing tobacco from his jacket pocket and returns to her chair on the stage. She is accompanied by a pale yellow Labrador who is noisily chewing a large bone; no attempt is made to quiet the dog. The lady has a board on her lap and is tying a fly—perhaps an elk hair caddis. The speaker, whose carriage and slenderness belie his years, smiles winningly at the ten or twelve people in the audience. He takes a sip from a glass containing a brown liquid—probably cough medicine— and begins, barely suppressing an appealing stutter.

THIS YEAR the Chairman has insisted that we keep the report at a higher level. Specifically, it has been requested that I not mention trap and skeet averages, poker games, or attempt—to use *her* words—any diversionary measures like turkey calls or demonstrations of the double haul. As is often the case, her ideas about riveting conversation and my own are not the same.

As you know, the news has been filled with various takeover schemes. Unfortunately, Management has misinterpreted the purpose of these moves and has insisted on total inventory control. As a minority stockholder, I have been asked to submit a complete listing of all equipment in excess of $100 in value. I have refused to do so until we can come to an agreement on the meaning of the word *value*. My point is that an object like a fly rod, that is ostensibly worth, say, $150 (or at least cost that much) is now worth considerably less since two guides are held on by plastic tape, one tip has a rather nasty set, and the rod varnish is nicked in many places. Not so, says Management, recalling as is her wont, the fact that I purchased the rod against her advice by claiming it to be an "investment." While I have no wish, believe me, to dwell on Management's sense of humor, I do think that the present standards are rather harsh. If time permits, I may well ask for a show of hands on this.

Although I have done everything humanly possible to allay the Chairman's suspicions that she has taken up with a spendthrift who is constantly coveting another shotgun or salmon reel, it seems that the situation is not far from a "critical mass," as a physicist might put it. Because it sets a bad precedent, I have reluctantly promised to make up a list of all equipment worth more than $100. But I will not permit the Chairman to conduct the inventory herself because she is well known for being unable to distinguish, for example, between guns actually owned, guns being held for others, or guns used for testing and scientific research. So let's move on to more agreeable subjects.

The half-white doe has happily come back with a new pair of plain-brown-wrapper fawns. The Canadas outdid themselves this past spring and we lost count of all the goslings. Admittedly, we spent most of the summer trying to stay downwind of the dogs! The pheasants are double what they were last year—still below what we'd like—and the evening symphony from the swamp roost is a lot louder and longer. The small covey of quail remains, heard but not seen. The owls flourish and the pond is continually dignified by the stately march of blue and white herons. The ospreys came back again for the summer and helped us out with the fishing.

Prudence and an opportune moment for spectacular savings resulted in the acquisition of two new fly rods ideal for salmon or saltwater. I'd like to have on the record that the Chairman accepted one without her usual song-and-dance on the subject of excessive numbers. Nor has she been noticeably shy about using one of the trap guns that once figured in her "driving us to the poorhouse" speech for which she is overly famous. And, should Management reconsider her unrealistic stance, there is a great possibility of the corporation obtaining, at a bargain-of-bargains price, a very nice 16-gauge side-by-side. However, if the Chairman were to get the equipment list she wants, she would immediately notice that a 16 gauge is already in the corporate inventory.

"Aha!" she would say. "I caught you—you don't *need another* 16-gauge shotgun!"

Unfortunately, Management has a history of being a bit short-sighted. Her longstanding reluctance to enter into intelligent discussion of choke boring, or to spend even a few hours reading Greener or Burrard on this fascinating subject, makes it difficult for me to explain that all 16 gauges, like hammers or shovels, are not alike. As you might recall from previous meetings, the present 16 gauge is improved cylinder and modified, while the needed acquisition is modified and full. Why does Management so casually dismiss these critical points of choke? I am sorry to say I have no sensible answer. All I can do is continue to press for arbitration, and I promise you that I will do just that.

At the moment, no other gun acquisitions are under consideration, with the exception of perhaps a .243, which is needed as a combination turkey and deer rifle. The subject has not been brought before the Chairman due to the present climate, so consider it tabled until the next meeting—unless, of course, a buy that is extremely advantageous to the corporation appears. If it does, you may contact me personally.

While there have been no major additions to inventory, neither have there been any losses, other than the usual miscellaneous items—shooting glasses, gloves, a box of assorted hoppers and elk hair caddis dries, and two sweaters whose absence coincided with the girls being home for Christmas.

In essence, the corporation is in good shape. Accordingly, I plan to make several requests of Management that involve the spring turkey season. Those of you who are turkey hunters will understand that the list may seem unreasonable or excessive to those who don't hunt turkeys, and will appreciate that I am facing some resistance. For instance, the Chairman, although she should know

better, has actually laughed out loud at my efforts to explain to her the difference between the needed tree bark camouflage and the leaf pattern that is already in inventory. I hesitate to even think about what is going to happen when we get to the subject of calls. The economy of bringing home a wild turkey as opposed to having to spend money for one may swing the Chairman to a more permissive mood. We shall see.

I see that the Chairman is looking at her watch, which means that we are about finished. If any of you have a few minutes, I'd be delighted to demonstrate how I took a right and a left on a covey rise on two occasions. Please feel free to join me on the stage.

The tall blonde woman takes the speaker in what appears to be a version of a police armlock and leads him into the wings. The audience, several of whom had to be vigorously awakened by their wives, drifts swiftly towards the exits. Two or three men start toward the stage but are pulled back by their wives. Sharp words are heard above the shuffling of feet and the phrase "never again" seems to be echoing in the hall.

○ *DEFINITIONS*

ABOUT THE TIME *FIELD & STREAM* had its beginnings, the market hunter played an important role in the scheme of things. Let's take a look at some common waterfowling words and see how their meanings have changed—in time or by necessity—since the heyday of market hunting.

Retrievers. To us, the modern wildfowlers, a Labrador or Chessie. To the market hunter, helpers in a rowboat. He called them "pick-up men."

A good night. For us, any one night we go to bed at a reasonable hour, without getting lathered in the clubhouse poker game or becoming too friendly with Jack D. To him, a full moon with a light layer of clouds, a bit of weather in the offing, and a good gunning lantern. Market hunters agreed that once they shot ducks against the light of the moon, shooting in broad daylight just wasn't the same.

Decoy. To the market hunter, preferably a live duck—a "caller"—in addition to a big stool of handcarved birds. Jester, Hudson, or Cobb would turn out several dozen for a few dollars when they had time off from gunning or boat-building. To us, probably plastic duck decoys, maybe half tires or stickups of plywood, but not something to dwell on a whole lot. The oldtimers said that the best *decoy* was a bushel of corn. I wouldn't know about that.

Limit. For the old gunner, when the birds stopped flying or he ran out of shells, or the boat was full of game. As for us, you don't have to ask. Most of us don't shoot a limit that often anyway—sometimes out of choice, sometimes not.

Waterproof. To us a "state of the art" camouflage parka, probably with a good warm synthetic filler. To him, a jacket coated with paraffin or tar. Actually, the word *waterproof* probably wasn't in his vocabulary.

Shells. Something the old market hunter paid up to a nickel apiece for if he didn't load his own, which he most likely did. I don't know what *you* paid for your last box of "magnums"; I'm trying to forget. Our shells are a lot better, if that's any consolation, and we don't need as many as he did. There are old stories about going through five or six hundred shells in a day. I seem to remember an oldtimer who brought back 578 ducks after 600 shots. I'm glad I didn't have to go up against *him* in the live-pigeon ring!

Lost. To them, someone was lost when he was blown out to sea or drowned; to me, lost means out of sight of land.

Duck call. To him, the sound made by a live black duck or mallard tethered to a stake at the edge of the decoy stool. To us, a plastic or wooden barrel with a reed. When certain people blow a duck call, it sounds like a duck, and that's skill. When I blow one, it's conservation!

Market. Where the old gunner sold his birds. A dollar and a half was a good price for a canvasback; blacks, redheads, etc., went for less. In some places the market gunning season went from September to March—there were worse jobs, lower in pay and prestige. Only two things kept me from market gunning: I was born too late and I shoot too poorly. But what a feeling it must have been to be sitting out in the bay with a couple of hundred shells at hand and the wind in just the right quarter!

Crab. One of the staples of the old bayman's diet. To us, crab is what our wives do after asking us where we've been when we said we'd be home right after dark.

Shotgun. To him, a tool. Probably 10-gauge, full-choked, 32-

inch damascus barrels and outside hammers. He probably spent less than $50 for the gun and could use it with the same skill that a shipwright had with adze and draw knife. To us it's a pump or semi-auto that costs hundreds; we tell ourselves it's an *investment.* We're not all that good with the gun, but probably won't admit it. I'm glad I don't have to rely on mine for a living; so is my family.

Knife. An edged instrument that the bayman used for everything from opening "rsters" to carving a new head for a decoy. To us, it's a device we paid too much for, is slightly dangerous in our hands, and is used mostly as a conversation piece or as the basis for an argument about sharpening methods.

Sculling. One of the waterman's battery of skills. He could scull a boat downwind into a flock of ducks before they knew he was

there. You can't do it with an outboard and besides it's illegal. I know two duck hunters who claim they know how to scull a boat. I believe one of them, partly.

Poling. Another almost lost art. I knew one old bayman who made his living, in part, cutting and selling poles. I asked him how he made out and he told that the demand wasn't too brisk. I've tried poling a few times, and for pure comedy it ranks just a little behind being on horseback. But a boat won't step on you if you fall off it.

Sinkbox. An old blind that was extremely effective. It ranks just below a coffin for comfort—and sometimes peace of mind.

Layout boat. This is usually not quite as comfortable to shoot out of as a sinkbox. If fish and game people had any common sense, they'd make the cutoff age for a layout boat occupant about twenty-five. There are a lot of things I like to do lying down, but shooting a shotgun isn't one of them.

Shore blind. A place from which to gun ducks. To the bayman, a shore blind was where you went if the bay was frozen or you just wanted woodies or black ducks. To us, a shore blind is built of brush or cedar or marsh grass. The best shore blinds are huge and often have wood stoves in them. When your steak is ready, the cook blows a duck call—the feeding call, of course—so it's important to recognize this.

A water blind works best as a nesting place for ospreys.

Weather. To the old hunter, weather was something you could hold in your hand or let run down the back of your neck. To us, *weather* is bad unless you want waterfowl. It has to have a 15- to 20-knot wind to give the right flavor. When you feel that you ought to have your head examined for just being outside, the weather's about perfect. Super perfect is when you speculate about what foreign country's shore the body will wash up on. Some oldtimers like to tell about days when the wind wouldn't let the anchor chain hit the water, but that's probably an exaggeration.

Season. To the old market gunner, it was when there were ducks—usually beginning in September and ending in March (most oldtime market gunners must have been bachelors). Today's seasons are largely in the hands of the Federal government. Some states regard this as a challenge and go into an area breakdown that defies any understanding at all. Being on the wrong side of a road or river can turn you into a criminal; so can steel shot zones, unless you're a qualified cartographer.

Species. Ducks come in different colors and sizes. The old-timer could handle this—usually he didn't care because it didn't make a lot of difference to him. Today, things are different thanks to the point system where the last bird you shoot is a hen—no matter what really happens. If you think you're good at separating species, try it in fog at dawn. When you've mastered that, try picking out the hen mallard from the black duck in an area where they interbreed. But don't do it over a gun barrel.

Lead. Sometimes called "forward allowances." This is like money—you seldom have enough of it. When you think you have a good idea of how far to point the muzzle in front of a duck, you can sit in the empty chair right next to the oldtimer. He always resisted any temptation to verbalize his ability with a shotgun; that is the definition of wisdom.

The list could go on and on. If you detect here some admiration for the old marketeer, you're right. It's true he shot too many for too long. But he didn't pollute the bays and waterways, he didn't kill the eelgrass, and he didn't drain and pave the breeding grounds and the feeding places. His time came and went, quickly, like the Mountain Man and the cowboy. I have, at one time or another, imagined myself as a market hunter (and Mountain Man and cowboy). Maturity and reality forced me to other means of livelihood. But, every so often, when I can see the ducks tolling in by the hundreds, I ask to be forgiven, or at least understood, for wishing to be out there in a sinkbox with a couple of hundred shells and my pick-up man watching from the dory.

One of my favorite things in life is Atlantic salmon fishing. This is the George River in Quebec, one of the most awesome stretches of water I've ever fished. But here are four fine reasons that this is one of the most unforgettable places I'll ever be.

○ *SPECIAL SPOTS*

A COMMON Indian belief held that every person needed a "sacred" spot, a place where one could be refreshed or made strong, or calmly think things out to a solution—a place where one felt happy and secure. The Japanese share this ancient belief in a lovely way by building little shrines, perhaps no more than a pair of sticks, at a place where they felt a moment of wonderment—at the way the light suddenly fell through a tree, or a bird singing in a tone that caught the heart.

Most of us build shrines in our own private ways. I've buried rifle shells in a few places because I just had to do *something* to celebrate and prolong my time of joy. I've built little stone cairns along the edges of brooks hoping that someday I might come back and remember happy times. And I've admired petroglyphs I've seen in the mountains, carved by some ancient soul whose moment of inspiration was, I like to think, a prayer of thanks in stone.

When I was an eight-year-old trapper, I found an old chestnut brought to the earth by worms. The hollow stump that was left was just right. When I climbed inside and stood up, I could look over the top and enjoy that delicious feeling of almost being invisible—I could see without being seen. I would slither inside that stump and think, and wonder, and guess, and wish. I was protected and comforted; this was my special *spot*, and I used it every chance I had.

There were other special spots. I had a summer spot on a huge rock that split a brook, where I could lay me down and listen to the water and think about where it came from, how it turned and curved and hushed itself and sometimes laughed or argued. And there was the old oak tree in which I would perch like a two-headed bird, stretched out along a limb that swung over a magic springhole like a bowsprit. I watched fish and ducks and the occasional loon, and sometimes I made faces at myself in the water's surface. I was warned not to go near that springhole because, so they said at the store, the place was quicksand and bottomless—guaranteed to whet the curiosity of a small boy. There were spots in haylofts, in countless climbing trees, and one under a bridge where I could enjoy the imaginary danger of cars running inches above me.

Like most kids, I had enough special spots scattered around so that refuge was always close at hand. And all my dogs would have

Obviously a posed picture of tarpon fishing in Islamorada. In the heat of battle I'd be standing on my line or have the fly embedded in the casting platform—or both.

to be considered special spots, because when I needed instant comfort I could always find it by wrapping my arms around them.

There are obvious special spots that offer comfort and solace—a duck blind, an old favorite deer stand, a stone wall where it's refreshing to sit and rest and mull over the day, a trout pool that offers more than just the promise of fish, an island of woods by a

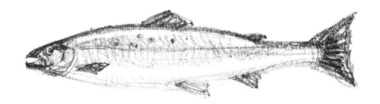

grainfield where the home covey lets you listen to its evening service. I have a place in the Florida Keys that's special to me because of my passion for tarpon fishing. And there's a corner of a porch on an old camp overlooking the Restigouche River that seems to sum up the inexplicable meaning of salmon fishing. When I'm there, I feel the magic like nowhere else. You might accept these special spots of mine without question, or you might not; the chemistry is often a surprise, like love at first sight.

The big brown trout has his spot beneath the cut bank where he's safe from ospreys and otters. The puppy has his spot under the porch where the big dogs won't bother him when he's tired and wants to be alone. The elk snuggles under the tilted pine that softens the wind, his bed deep and rank and comforting.

Not long ago a puppy came into my life and I wanted to do something to let her know that I knew she was very special. So I stretched out on the bed and became her special spot. She recognized it instantly. Her small head slid underneath my chin and she tucked one tiny arm under mine and went to sleep. She was where she belonged, protected not by my strength or size, but merely by my presence—I was the right thing in the right spot to soothe her.

A special spot is both physical and transcendental; you don't look for it as much as you believe in it. Great music can create a spot, and so can a calling loon or the northern lights. These kinds of spots are an epiphany of sorts, something that gladdens the heart with a sudden recognition—the creaking of a tree against the wind, the sound of rain, watching a muskrat carrying a fresh-picked supper for her babies.

I hope that whatever special spots you have will bring you beauty and a touch of wildness and peace and understanding.

○ *MOUSETRAPS*

I WAS RUMMAGING in one of the storage closets in my shed trying to find a box of 28-gauge 8's. I don't remember what I wanted them for now, but I suspect it was one of my make work organizing schemes that I use as a frequent excuse to avoid sitting in front of a typewriter.

I had found a bonus—a forgotten box of 16-gauge 5's—and was looking for more of those when I saw the mouse flicker from one corner of the closet to the other. Moving a couple of Ranger shell boxes, I found the remnants of an old wool army scarf that I once favored for duck hunting. Long forgotten, like most of the things in this out-of-the way wooden pocket, it had been altered into a king-sized bed about 3 inches or so wide.

My first reaction was thoughtless instinct; I found myself back in the main house looking for one of the little wooden mousetraps left over from the period when I attempted to keep the dogs off the living room furniture. I baited the trap with bacon frosted with peanut butter and, back in the shed, slid it onto the closet shelf and closed the door.

I waited around for a while listening, with quickly diminishing expectations, for the doomsday fall of the wire jaw. But it didn't take long for me to admit that my heart was far from warm about my trapping expedition. My shed, where my office is, has squirrels in the attic, garter snakes in the crawl space, starlings nesting on the sliding doors, wrens under the eaves, and is an ark for all sorts of insects—not to mention the odd dog who resides there. To object to a creature as small as a field mouse was ridiculous. The closet is a junk shop, and if I were honest, I'd admit that the presence of a decent, hard-working mouse might even give the place a little class. I went back and sprung the trap, leaving it there with the hope the peanut butter and bacon would do for an apology.

It's not that I'm especially fond of mice, but somehow the thought of the one mouse bedded down in my old scarf carried a certain feeling of live-and-let live that made me feel a lot more comfortable than I had listening for the neck-snapping crack of the trap. If it turned out that I was running a mouse hotel, I could always get the cat. Her presence alone would be enough to make them leave. This was no doubt the thing to do if eviction became necessary; both the cat and I would get some personal satisfaction from it. But right now this was just my mouse—a single fellow waiting for Miss Right to come along, or an old fellow waiting for someone else.

The next day when I went to retrieve my muted trap, most of the little brown scraps of wool were gone. My tenant had up and

moved, as I have done myself several times, looking for a more tranquil place and more understanding, or more distant neighbors. No doubt overly influenced by *The Wind In The Willows* and Mr. Disney, I felt bothered about his absence. I stood there, my mind filling with charmingly drawn, color sketches of my mouse packing his khaki scraps in a tiny red bandanna, adjusting his cap, and then, after lighting his pipe in a show of manly bravado, setting off fearlessly on a new road that might prove somewhat perilous, but with a happy ending guaranteed.

I untied the bit of bacon scrap and fed it to Maggie, who had been watching this whole operation with keen interest. Then I cleaned the trap and put it on my desk as a clip for letters yet unanswered—much more functional than using it to keep Labradors off the orange sofa.

A few days later, in another closet across the hall, I found my box of 28-gauge shells—9's, not the 8's I had so clearly remembered. But I'm used to things turning up when I least expect them. Actually, I hadn't been looking for shells this time; I'd been poking around hoping to find another king-sized bed made from a handful of khaki tatters.

○ *SKETCHES OF QUAIL COUNTRY*

ALL ACROSS THE SOUTH you'll find little cabins tucked away here and there underneath the pines. There won't be much of a yard, but as often as not there's some sort of dog run and almost always a two- or three-horse stable. A stone here or there with Dixie or Lady or Luke crudely chiseled on it marks the place where an old friend rests—a soft-footed singles dog or a barrel-chested pointer with a range like the wind.

Inside there'll be the faded pictures—men on horseback, with their wide-brimmed hats pulled down over their eyes, kneeling by a bird dog and cradling its proud head in prouder hands; a boy with what is surely his first gun, a man with one just as surely his last. A woman, elegant in flared breeches and a flowing tie, holds a sleek 20-bore that she obviously has mastered. Old calendars still tell the days of a long-ago bird season, holding time back to a year when things were better, before the oak tree found its way through the porch floor and there were still enough bricks in the chimney.

On the outside the cabin looks tattered and shameful; its useful time has largely gone, hastened by the coming of the car. "Town is only a few minutes away, why waste money fixing up the roof and porch?" And, of course, they don't.

Inside there is an old refrigerator, one of those made in a time when everything seemed to run forever, and a plain gray enamel stove that never gave anyone trouble. An oilcloth-covered table and three mismatched chairs rest on the linoleum floor with the usual buckles in the usual treacherous places; in the corner sits an old armchair with rusted springs coiled like snakes, rescued from the sideyard by someone.

I find myself curiously drawn to this cabin, wishing we were both younger, with stronger, sleeker porches and foundations not yet tilted by wind and frost. I guess we don't have time for cabins the way we used to. In their day, they provided warmth and welcome shelter, a place for the good talk before the hunt and the reflections afterwards.

Nearby, the small stables still bear little crudely lettered signs above the lopsided Dutch doors: *Patches, Soot, Tinker.* Inside,

hanging on homemade nails and forked sticks, are what time and mice have left of the stirrups and bridles. I pick up a tarnished bit from the littered floor, steal it into my pocket, and find it strangely comforting. But before I go, I put it on a doorside shelf, hoping that someone who remembers how Patches loved a handheld carrot or apple will take it home.

The kennel is overgrown now, like an untended garden, its wire fence as flimsy as lace. But it's not hard to imagine the great-chested pointers throwing themselves against it in frustrated frenzy as the gunning parties walked around admiring those bulging eyes and rippling flanks, and the pure, singular, demonic, born-to-hunt hellishness. (A lot of the old bird hunters I've known weren't a whole lot different, but I was never so foolish as to make that observation out loud!)

While the horses were being readied, the men would stand around, drinking one more cup of coffee and chatting about the weather and how wild the birds were getting. The dog handler would pick out the morning crew, and as the left-behinds howled and kicked the dirt with their hind feet, he lifted his favorites by the scruff and the hindquarters and popped them into the coops on the dog wagon. And then, like ducks lifting off a pond, men, horses, and the dog wagon were suddenly off together without much being said about it. If there's a more delicious moment than this, the starting out, almost knightlike, of a quail hunt, I surely don't have any idea what it could be.

The first brace of dogs and the outrider—the scout—are almost instantly out of sight, but not matter; our rendezvous are laid out almost like a map. We'll visit the Cemetery covey first and see if anybody's home. Then we'll stop by Burnt Pine, Sawmill, and Outhouse, and a final sweep along the edges of the swamp ought to have us back at the cabin by lunchtime.

From far off you can hear the scout singing to the dogs; when we stop to listen for the call of *point*, the cardinals fill in the quiet. Two guns get down and wordlessly separate, one sliding to the right, the other taking the left. The dog handler is purposely casual and leisurely; his dogs will hold quietly and he's bragging on it. At the flush there are four shots, and three birds fall. One gunner casually clears the smoke from his double; the other throws his head back, rolls his eyes, and smiles as he flips one of the empties at the handler: "Save that one, I want to send it back to the factory and tell them it's no good."

The road turns back toward home as it always must. Up ahead, before the little white cabin comes into view, you can hear singing; it contrasts nicely with the sweet soft smell of frying chicken and the harsh shouts of the kenneled dogs—"Me next, me next!"

The handler reins his horse and slides out of the saddle. You walk alongside trying to memorize, to hold forever, just the way Jake is standing with Molly a little to one side honoring so tensely she's shivering. Then you walk in between the dogs.

If it goes exactly the way it ought to, there'll be a single quail haloed in the sun against a background of pines and you'll press this picture like a flower between the pages of your mind. In the silence you hold the bird in both hands and look at it. From a distance a person might think they saw you saying a little prayer, the way good and honest hunters sometimes do when they think they're unobserved.

○ *BON APPETIT!*

PEOPLE ALWAYS ask me about the famous eateries I find in my travels and what the cuisine is like. So here are a few typical places I've reviewed for your traveling pleasure. Enjoy!

SEÑOR CYRIL'S

Somewhere, Mexico

Atmosphere: There is basically post-Aztec, but it's hard to tell how much. There are no lights to speak of, not for old-world charm, but to prevent the guests from seeing the variety and quantity of insects, reptiles, and serpents that live in the nooks and crannies—not excluding your shoes and socks. The centerpiece of the main foyer sets the tone.

It features an artfully arranged group of large pitchers rumored to contain a beverage mixing equal parts of tequila, lime juice, and Triple Sec. It has a Spanish name, which I think starts with "M."

Recommended dishes: The health addict would do well to confine himself to the canned pineapple juice and the fresh bread. There are frequent dishes on the menu that bear familiar names: Chili Rellenos, fried doves, hamburger, and chicken. This will calm the fears of the casual observer, but the sophisticated traveler will have noted that the countryside abounds in roadrunners, magpies, and some sort of marmot. Tucked in the back of his head is the unsettling fact that rattlesnake meat is white and is thought to resemble the flavor of chicken.

Breakfast is the usual coffee and Rolaids, universal in all camps that cater to the hunter, as is the lunch of a beer or two and, for those of iron constitution, a small portion of nachos. Dinner is, in large part, the liquid from the previously mentioned centerpiece. To suggest straying from the known, in its strictest sense, would be foolhardy.

Hours: Food is served whenever someone gets around to cooking, which in the Mexican idiom, translates as *who cares.* A working knowledge of Spanish might help, but I doubt it. Food is always served after dark, for which you should be thankful.

Credit cards: None. Señor Cyril runs this as a retreat, a place of quiet and meditation. Donations are accepted provided they are no more than a tenth of your annual income or your net worth, whichever is the larger.

Dress code: Governed more by the omnipresent Cacti and rattlesnakes than good taste or stylish trends. It is impossible to offend Sr. Cyril, who sets a rather loose tone.

STANLEY'S

Pearsall, Texas

Atmosphere: Noisy; there is often a fight going on, which is sometimes obscured by a quarrelsome card game. Nonsmokers are requested to take their trade elsewhere.

Recommended dishes: Anything you personally see come from a can, like tuna fish. Cereals are okay too. Fried chicken is often edible if you get it before the house sauce is added, as is the catfish. The rest of the menu is "spicy," which means toxic unless you were raised on a variety of chili peppers. The beverage is Lone Star—you have a choice of cans or bottles. They also serve coffee, but don't stir it with a plastic spoon.

One of the quaint customs is "Stanley's Chili Challenge." The host serves you a bowl and then adds tablespoons of Tabasco until you say *stop.* He then serves himself an identical dish. If he can't finish his without a beverage, you eat free. If you lose, you pay double. I understand he put himself through law school eating flies and jalapeños. You don't beat a man at his own game.

Hours: The place never closes. The bar is always open.

Credit Cards: None. Cash only unless you have a house account; you can open one if you know the A & M fight song or can imitate a javelina.

Dress code: Never remove your hat.

JIMMY'S SNACKS

Clinton, New Jersey

Atmosphere: To be charitable, call it slovenly. If you take your eyes off your plate, one of the countless dogs is likely to clean it for you. Don't be surprised if your glass has hair in it—same for the ice cubes.

Recommended dishes: The standby is a variety of flavored popcorn or imitation cheese things that look like plastic worms. (If you always wondered who bought that stuff, now you know.) Another feature is a selection of spiced sausages served cold accompanied by an obscure commercial dip that must have been a rejected C-ration of some sort.

Until noon the house specialty is a version of Huevos Rancheros. I can't comment on this as I have always gone with the peanut butter and jelly on toast. I could describe what it looks like, but I won't. The most popular beverage is Cuba Libre. Try one, if you must, out of curiosity, but there is usually a good supply of little-known, inferior Spanish wines—stick with those. A refreshing touch is the house tradition of serving a small bowl of antacid tablets—take a handful for later!

Hours: All night, featuring highland bagpipe music after 2 A.M.

Credit Cards: None. Cash or barter is the system here. Trout flies, shotgun shells, old knives—almost anything of a sporting nature—although I have no idea what the proprietor does with them.

Dress code: About what you'd choose if you were cleaning a plugged drain or changing a truck tire.

FAMOUS FRED'S

New Brunswick, Canada

Atmosphere: A cut above the average log cabin, but the host wants to keep reminding you that you're "roughing it." If you're ever homesick for your old drill instructor, this is the place for you! It's the rare lady guest who doesn't learn a new phrase or an interesting twist on an old one—but that's part of the charm.

Recommended dishes: Now that the proprietor has been banished from the kitchen, the food is surprisingly good. None of the "old hands" really miss porcupine, or bear stew, or some of the less readily identifiable cuisine of the past.

I won't dwell on the trail lunches, since you *can* survive without them, but the traditional tea poured from an old tin can is still guaranteed to give a start to your dentist when you get back home. Take a tip from an oldtimer and just drink it—don't watch it being made or poured!

Hours: Breakfast is served shortly following the after-dinner cordials. There is often entertainment, if that word can dignify a group of overweight men stomping their feet to a monotone fiddler or a serenade of off-color infantry ballads from World War II.

Credit cards: The management will accept almost anything, but is always delighted with cash.

Dress code: Most of the time you have to wear something. War surplus is considered acceptable, and a common touch is to have the pants "stagged" by a chain saw or an ax. This can be, and often is, done on the premises.

HAYWIRE BOB'S

Ft. Worth, Texas

Atmosphere: This eatery has been described, not unreasonably, as appealing to the criminally insane. Although frequented by a variety of professional men, the general ambiance is probably not much different from a frontier station at the end of a cattle drive.

Recommended dishes: If you stay with commercially baked pies and cakes you can't go wrong. Don't take anyone's word that the red and green things are vegetables—I don't know what they are, but I do know they're smuggled in from interior Mexico. All the food is prepared in glass cookware, if that's a clue.

I've learned to prepare everything myself, and then only salads. I try to avoid having any sauce touch my bare skin. I know that the salad dressing will take the blue off a gun barrel and that the coffee will eat through fly line coating. If you're starving and you're a third generation native to the region, you're on your own. Don't say you weren't warned. Part of the sport at Haywire Bob's is watching a non-Texan eat, or try to.

I can and do recommend the liquid refreshments. The host is an outstanding supplier in both quality and quantity. One exception is the local Bloody Mary. The trick is to drink it before the bottom comes out of the plastic cup. Then *cold soup* is also famous; served on ice and garnished with an olive or a twist of lemon rind, it is redolent of juniper.

Hours: The service is a continuous buffet. If any particular dish is in short supply, the host adds a pint of home-brewed hot sauce, which eliminates the casual snacker. When you're hungry, eat, but you'd better be hungry.

Credit cards: None. This place is run on the honor system, and if you stay up long enough, the host will forget your name. He makes it up on the betting games that are part of the shooting and fishing, or so I'm told.

Dress code: I can't imagine anything, short of a coat and tie, that would be considered out of place. If you're wearing a dress, you'd better be a woman.

This is just a sampling of the more exotic eateries that I see in a year's travel. Of course these are the cream, but that's obvious. I've not rated them one (★) or two (★★) or three stars (★★★) like most critics do, since all of these eateries are chosen out of necessity. Because they're well off the beaten track, they can get by with somewhat less in the way of creature comforts and niceties than other places with lower standards, but only to be with certain close friends.

I did forget one thing—if you're going to try any of these spots, bring your own napkins and silverware, and especially your own glass. And maybe a note from your doctor. One more word of advice—don't mention my name. It won't help. None of the proprietors read much more than the usual notices they get from the Board of Health.

Bon appetit!

○ *BINGO*

THEY WERE BOTH too fat. He had a big safety pin, the kind used for a horse blanket, holding the front of his hunting coat, and under that an old red-and-green wool shirt that threatened to throw its buttons. His black Labrador wheezed and whistled from an effort of walking up to the line where the judges were waiting, and when he removed her collar, her neck fell to double in size. As they stood there listening to the explanation of the test, the fat black dog snuggled so close to her master's leg that she seemed to be leaning on him for support. He let his arm drop and she put her nose in his palm and closed her eyes. A minute ago I had been ready to laugh at these two, but now I had to turn for a minute and wipe away something that seemed to have gotten into my eyes.

The test wasn't easy. The first bird was a rather long blind across a weedy channel and the second mallard was a long marked single deep back among dead timber. A couple of the younger dogs had finished the series, but none without a lot of whistles and hand signals. On a rating of one to ten, the best score I had given was a generous five. A lot of duck hunters would have used a boat rather than send a dog through the stumps and snags, and I wouldn't have blamed them. What we judged had meant to be a hard marking test turned out to be one that depended a lot on pure heart; "want to" was what we ended up grading the dogs on. Most of them didn't have a lot of it.

The fat dog's name was Bingo, and somehow I got the picture

of the two of them eating popcorn together and watching game shows on television. I imagined them sitting side by side at the local bar, drinking beer and watching baseball. What I couldn't imagine is one ever being more than three feet from the other if they could help it.

Much to my surprise and delight, Bingo did a pretty respectable job on the long blind. You could hear her for half a mile, huffing her slow way through the lotus pads and pickerel weed. At first I was worried that she'd drown or have a heart attack, but she was too fat to sink and seemed more than delighted to do something that her boss wanted done. Bingo struggled her belly over the bank, took a half dozen deep breaths, waddled over and picked up the duck and swam back. Her master hadn't used one whistle or so much as moved a hand. It took forever, but Bingo was showing the skinny Labs a thing or two and the crowd loved every long, worried minute of it.

She finished her retrieve with a lovely little flourish, walking around behind and sort of adjusting herself and then sitting practically on his foot and offering him the duck as if it were a crown. As one of the senior judges. I was supposed to be the very model of impartiality and decorum, but I put my notebook under my arm and joined the gallery in a spontaneous minute of applause. Then I wrote "10" next to Bingo's name on my scorecard. By now she'd recovered her breath and her handler signaled that he was ready for the next test. He had Bingo lined up perfectly and she slowed with anticipation at the shot. The bird boy threw the shackled duck and Bingo slid into the water with a very audible sigh of pleasure and began paddling toward the swamp.

You look for a lot of subtle things when you're judging a trial. You get so you can sense indecision in a dog, or reluctance. Some dogs are too bold and don't use their head, just crash on until they stumble over a bird or get handled to it. Others are too tentative, continually asking their handler, "Am I doing this right?" I don't like either one. What I like in a dog is a mixture of confidence, common sense, and obedience; about in that order. I'm big on a good dashing water entry, an aura of determination, and a feeling that a dog wants to please rather than do the job like an automaton. I like to see more of the pure dog than just the result of training.

I'd gotten away from field trials for a while because I felt that a lot of the judging was unrelated to hunting situations, and there was a laziness that ended up with the tests being too hard rather than being fair, and having a few dogs come back in recalls. I'd run

a lot of dogs and had a very sensitive feeling about the work and companionship part of it, and I hated to drop a dog too quickly. I'd lost a couple of first place ribbons because of what I felt was a lack of understanding of the dogs' problems in certain situations. I felt that a lot of judges had never really done enough gunning or worked enough with dogs to be able to get a good handle on borderline judgements.

But, at the bottom, the whole thing is for the dog, not the convenience of the gallery or the handlers or the judges. You get to feeling sorry for dogs that have handlers who are too harsh on them—and almost as often, for handlers who have dogs that are too good for them. I'd been one of the latter a couple of times and am still a little embarrassed about being obviously dumb when I should have left it all to the dog. But here I was trying to keep a good balance between my head and my heart and worrying about poor old Bingo running into an underwater log or limb and getting disoriented, or worse, hurt.

Bingo had been her perfunctory self in our other series in the morning, taking forever and looking anything but stylish or fiery, but somehow she always got the job done. Other dogs were faster, more elegant, or more exciting, but where they'd overrrun a bird, then circle for a minute trying to find it, Bingo would walk up to exactly where it was, pick it up, and come back. One of the gallery remarked that watching her was "as exciting as seeing a guy lay brick." That may be, but the brick got laid, and laid right. And after all, this was just a fun interclub trial, not a big regional AKC sanctioned affair. We were supposed to be judging hunting retrievers, not watching a track meet. And as much as I like a dog that can zip out and zip back in, I also respect the old workman who gets it done right the first time.

Bingo was not going to be placed first or second. Those places had already been established by a couple of dogs that were clearly "big trial" contenders, dogs that shouldn't have been in this trial at all. It was just that their owners were ribbon-hungry and liked to show off a bit when the chance came along. But a third here was not to be taken lightly. There were plenty of old campaigners doing their stuff, and a couple of up-and-coming dogs that had it all on any given day.

Sometimes in competitions, a great and certain knowledge spreads among the judges, the spectators, and the contestants that a prize is deserved, regardless of what the rules or the score are. And there was poor old Bingo, looking like the kid at the picnic who had unexpectedly been asked to join the games and said, "Why not?"

Well, not to prolong what you've already guessed. Bingo did it all, and we gave her the ribbon for third place with as much pleasure and sense of rightness as I can ever remember.

At the little awards ceremony, her master poured her tiny mouthfuls of beer from a long-necked bottle, and Bingo seemed rather self-satisfied. I was in love with her by now and more than a little envious of her owner. When it was his turn to come up and get his ribbon we all burst into a few minutes of applause and cheering that we had held, pent up, for some time. He took the ribbon and waited until we'd quieted down, then bent over and fastened it to Bingo's collar, played with her ear for a second and, speaking for both of them said "Well, as they used to say, the show ain't ever over until the fat lady sings."

Then he and the fat lady went over to his truck. He lifted her into the front seat and gave her the last swallow out of the beer bottle, handed the empty to a friend who came to say good-bye, and they drove off.

I watched the truck disappear as it turned through a stand of pines and, through the rear window, I could see them sitting shoulder to shoulder. For a moment I thought about love. Not the kind that they sing about or the kind that disgraces a bumper sticker, but the kind that means you'll put your arm in the fire. The kind that becomes a Navy Cross or Silver Star—or a ten-cent pink and silver ribbon. The kind that you don't talk about. The kind that is just there, like the Earth.

I wasn't the only one watching the truck fade away. Half a dozen of the crowd had moved off by themselves and were watching it too. I wondered what we all felt in common, and I think it was sorrow. Suddenly we all knew what it was we had been looking for for so long, from someone or something . . . and we felt that it had passed us by.

I hesitate to caption this since I am about as burdened as a knight in armor and have just conquered a rather less than bragging size foe. No, I do not look disappointed; resigned is a better word; I have been here before and will be here again. On the bright side—I didn't set skunked!

○ THE RIGHT WORD

I'VE ALWAYS BEEN curious about why words have different meanings for different people.

Take the word *late*. If your buddy promised to pick you up at 5:30 for a duck hunt, and he doesn't arrive until 5:45, you're not only frantic with worry—you're very annoyed because he's *late*. That evening, after the shooting is over, you and your buddy are enjoying a refreshment. He casually asks you what time you told your wife you'd be home. You say, 7:30-ish.

"It's after 8 now," he tells you.

"Okay, I'll call and tell her we'll be a little late," you say. You might even do it. But note how the concept of *late* differs. It would be only honest to bring in the wife's point of view. But then, nobody ever said that life was fair.

We all know the first words you hear from a child are "I'm busy," when he, she, or it is addressed by a parent with a chore in mind. But that same child has never been busy when the phone rings.

It's in this manner that words lose their true meanings and take on selective definitions according to the user.

Example: you rarely hear the word "missed" at a trap shoot. The scorer calls "lost," which has the ancient connotation of something happening beyond one's control—some outside force is involved. Targets are "dropped," "got away," "fooled me," or some other phrase that implies evil intent on the part of the target to humiliate the shooter. Another example: there are thousands of bad rifles,

*Famous as a story-teller, I have
Capt. Jimmie Albright breathless as I
describe losing a tarpon.*

but I never heard anyone even hint that he wasn't a good rifleman. Rifles are often "off"—a lovely and mysterious abstraction—but this has no relation whatsoever to human error.

Since words can be elastic, we've all learned the hard way to be precise in phrasing questions, taking into account all the variables we can—the person(s), the time, and the place.

Let's say you are dove hunting in Arizona. You ask one of the local gunners: "Do you see many snakes around here?" He'll likely say: "No." The critical word here is *many*. To me or you, one snake is *many;* to the Arizonan, many could really be many more than one.

Let's say you are duck hunting and, for some reason, want to get out of the boat. You might well make the mistake of asking: "Can I step out here?" A very polite guide will say: "You sure can, if you want." What you sought and found is permission; what you really wanted to know was the depth of the water, which you found out all by yourself, the hard way. To a Maine duck hunter who enjoys gunning on ice-covered, off-shore rocks, a "cool spell" is entirely different than a cool spell is to a cracker who has never seen ice that didn't come from a machine.

I've learned a lot the hard way. Once, when I'd waded across a big river and fished for a while, I started wading back. My guide watched me start, then suggested I wait until he got the boat for me. I replied smartly that I got over, so I could certainly get back. What he'd noticed, and I hadn't, was that while the water may be deeper in some places than others, it's about the same temperature all over.

I've noticed that more and more people are becoming more careful of their speech. A few years ago, I was shooting pheasants in England and got into a conversation with one of the beaters during the lunch break. He seemed extraordinarily well-spoken, so I complimented him on his delightful use of the language. He smiled, and said: "I suppose it comes from being a professor of poetry at Oxford for so many years!"

Another problem with words is distance. Not one guide in a hundred, and certainly no casual gunner, has the vaguest idea of how far a mile is on a log road. In my experience, it's about a mile and a half or two in the West, and about half to three-quarters of a mile in the East. When I get lost in Colorado or Wyoming, it's because I didn't walk far enough; in Maine or Vermont, it's the other way around. My solution is to walk about 15 minutes and stay put. I know I'm not where I'm supposed to be, but I'm close. I also know that deer or birds will cross where they're supposed to and that I won't be there. The guide will mutter something about "outdoor writer," and smile to himself. (Why a writer for an outdoor magazine is supposed to be a blend of Jim Bridger, Fred Kimble, and Admiral Perry, I really don't know. I've tried on countless occasions to explain that an outdoor writer spends most of his time writing instead of dashing around with Lewis & Clark, giving casting exhibitions, or running 100 straights at trap on weekends, but no one seems to understand.)

The worst judges of distance, aside from high handicap golfers, are rifle shooters. A man points to a sheep head on his wall and says he took the animal at about 400 yards. While I don't think I've ever had the courage to laugh, out loud, at such talk, I have on several occasions marveled at such shooting skill and mentioned that 400 yards is ten skeet fields back to back, a very good drive in golf, etc. But I guess that every rifleman has to have the odd 400 yarder, just like every fly rodder has to have a few casts that not only use the whole fly line, but tug out some of the backing, too. I suppose, in conversation, I just *might* have taken a duck or goose at 60 yards or so. But I do it in the spirit of things, not to prove my shooting skills, but merely to affirm how little I think of the 36-inch yard or the 16-ounce pound.

Since weights and measures are constantly used with a little artistic freedom, why should the concept of time be spared? There are various kinds of conversational time. One is the time a big fish is on; my estimate is about 20 minutes to the hour. Crawling while stalking a deer or an elk is about the same. The time you'll be home is the opposite—7 P.M. means 8:30 at the earliest. "I'm just going to fish for an hour" can cover two or two-and-and-a-half hours.

Time and distance depend strictly on the desirability of the destination. A 50-mile drive to visit your wife's cousin takes a minimum of two hours. A 50-mile drive to a woodcock cover only takes a half hour. An acre of lawn takes an hour to cover pushing a lawnmower, while an acre of bird cover can be worked, length and breadth, in fifteen minutes.

I don't believe any retriever has ever brought back a duck that

fell less than "a couple of hundred yards." And the average period of time that a bird dog is on point pushes half-an-hour.

There ought to be come kind of Sportsman's Almanac that converts weights and measures and time from "actual" to "conversational"—there's nothing wrong with a standard. I caught a rainbow trout last year in Idaho that measured 23 inches. But the measurement was hurried as I put the fish back, so some allowance ought to be made. I've been saying that the trout was 26 inches, but I've had this nagging doubt that I'm on the short side and not getting credit where credit is due. I also shot a deer that the guide said was around 250 yards away, but the shot was uphill and in the fog. I don't know how to add fog, but I know, from being a good listener, that uphill is worth another 25 yards and that numbers should always be rounded off. That would make it a 300-yard shot. I'll leave it at that and let the fog slide for the time being.

Just one last example of communications and I'll let you steelhead fishermen go back to working out your average length of cast in furlongs.

It seems that two hunters working the same bird field met and began to chat. The first hunter remarked that the pointer that had been working their way was a pretty good-looking dog. When the dog joined them, the first hunter asked the other: "Does your dog bite?" The man answered: "No siree!" The man who had asked the question reached over to pat the dog on the head and got a handful of teeth for his trouble.

"I thought you said your dog didn't bite," he said with more than a little surprise and anger in his voice.

The other hunter just smiled and said: "That ain't *my* dog."

*I think this was my first Arizona dove
shoot and by my satisfied expression I may
have worried one down; my normal dove
shooting look is one of puzzlement,
or perhaps embarrassed resignation especially
if I am reduced to borrowing more shells.*

○ *LABOR OF LOVE*

I SAW A PICTURE the other day in a magazine of a Labrador wearing a Ducks Unlimited cap and necktie, and holding, though not smoking, a pipe. No doubt you've seen Labs with sunglasses or a Lab at the tiller of an outboard, at the wheel of a pickup truck, and so on. None of this surprises me, since the Labrador was put on earth to show man what he might aspire to—loyalty, dedication, competence, and the ability to maintain a sense of dignity and good humor at the same time.

The sooner we become intelligent enough to really communicate with the breed on an equal level, the better off we'll be. After all, a Lab is the perfect fishing companion, an ideal partner for visiting country saloons, a never-bored buddy for a long trip, a creature whose tastes in music embraces it all from Willie Nelson to Wolfgang Amadeus Mozart.

Not that Labradors, like ourselves, are faultless. In their eagerness to please or help out, they often get a little ahead of us by not waiting until the whole scheme is laid out. For example, one of my salmon-fishing friends figured that since the Lab was once used to help haul nets, it could easily be trained to help land fish. He had probably seen pictures or heard stories of a Lab retrieving fish.

I'm not sure how he broached the idea to Duchess, but the method in his madness was flawed. I was there when, after he'd lost several fine fish, he began the process of *debriefing,* if that's the word to describe a month of thrashing a dog with a graphite rod, trying to net a fish without netting the dog when they are both occupying the same space in the water, etc. After several near capsizes, I had the temerity to ask him why he simply didn't go fishing without Duchess for a while so she might lose interest in being used as a living gaff. His gruff answer was typical of the dedicated retriever man: "She's my dog and I never go anywhere without her!"

I never had much luck getting any of my dogs to branch out and take over small chores like getting the paper, carrying shells along the trapline, or holding my pipe. Most of the time I had children who would occasionally do those things but they lacked the attention span of a Lab, and I could never really get them to come when they were called. I admit it was stupid, but I did train one dog to unlock a complicated kennel latch; the replacement latch was expensive and so complicated *I* had trouble opening it. I taught another Lab to run through a closed screen door, which at the time I thought was open. It's the only time I ever taught a dog to do something perfectly in a single lesson.

It's my personal theory that Labs are so eager to please they're constantly on the *qui vive* to discover what you need done and then do it—although their reasoning may not be perfectly clear to a human being until he gives the situation a lot of thought. My beloved Maggie began chewing holes in my office rug after I specifically asked her not to do so. Knowing how deep obedience runs in the breed, I puzzled over her behavior until it finally came to me: she had seen me practicing with my wedge and removing a small piece of carpet in the process. Maggie realized that a golf club was nothing compared to her destructive powers; why should the boss waste his time doing by inches what she could do by the sqaure foot. I taught another Lab to retrieve golf balls, never dreaming that one day cruel fate would see me living close to a golf course. Summer weekend mornings could be hell, especially for players who weren't familiar with the rules dealing with *outside interference.* Tippy finally got bored with golf, saving me from having to sell the house.

The aforementioned Maggie, being deeply sports-minded, was also fond of fly fishing in the extreme; well, not *exactly* fly fishing but more the challenge of teaching me the virtues of a high back-cast by catching the line on a low one. After I had ordered my Xth line, a friend asked me "What do you do with all these? Feed them to the dog?"

"Lucky guess," I told him, "lucky guess."

Over the years I've been keeping a list of good reasons to keep a Labrador; the number now stands at 654. There are also several good reasons not to keep a Lab, one of which is that if a robber falls over your dog in the dark and hurts himself, he can probably sue you.

Several of my friends have written books on training Labradors, and while my dogs enjoyed looking at the pictures, they felt the text was too complicated for most dog men to follow. I asked one of them, I think it was Maggie, if she thought she could do better. Being female, she asked if there was any money in it. I told her that we all write for the pure joy of it and that money taints the profession; this belief is very strongly held by publishers.

"I have better things to do with my time, in that case," she said.

"Like what?" I replied. "Spreading garbage all over?"

"Isn't that what you do most of the time?" she answered.

My reply was devastatingly witty and precisely to the point, and I'd tell you what it was except I've run out of space. But make that number 653, not 654.

A two-handed salmon rod is difficult to learn to use, but it's a god-send for long cast on a windy day. Some may feel the costume is a little eccentric; however, I am convinced I do much better casting the two-handed giant on European waters when I'm properly attired.

○ *HOROSCOPES*

ORDINARILY, I WELCOME the new year with my carefully considered horoscopes. But after studying the conjunctions and influences of the major planets, constellations, and stars, the results were so universally promising and cheerful that I decided against prying too deeply. I didn't want to discover that a Taurus would have a lower trap average and an indifferent year of trout fishing. All in all, this seems to be a good year just to be around. Only a handful of you, Capricorns for the most part, will have problems with waders and canoes. I see a new equipment phase for Libras, nothing extravagant, which will prove immensely helpful—probably a worming rod and a better reel, and possibly a new auto in 20 gauge that will be perfect for doves and quail.

It seems to be the perfect year for Aquarians to start a new puppy and for Pisces to start playing a little looser in games of seven card stud. A little less conservatism will be the prevailing mood for Aries. This will improve both your skeet average and the number of fish you catch—everybody hangs a fly in a tree or a plug on a stump now and then. Geminis have a lot of travel in the future with excellent results. I see a touch of romance but cannot tell whether it's a rifle or a redhead—with your luck it could be both! Those born under the sign of Cancer will be let off by state troopers with only a warning. Leos will likely dominate the Grand American and/or the local trap club. Start reloading early—you'll be in plenty of shootoffs! Virgos tend to be born big-game hunters, and an unusual season may be in store—be prepared to make a modest speech. Scorpios enjoy collecting stuff and there will be a bonus coming around the end, of August—watch for a yard sale about 20 miles from home and go early. Sagittarians only have an outstanding year about one out of three, and this is it. Those who wish to lose weight will find it easy, and a loved one will insist that you treat yourself to something special—the first letter seems to be a "P" and it's a shotgun made in Italy.

You'd think that anyone who has this gift of reading horoscopes would take advantage of it himself, but that wouldn't be fair. I will continue to fish when the water is too high and pick up my trap gun when the stars shudder at the very thought of it. My true destiny has yet to reveal itself, but the most encouraging thing is that I'm too old for child labor.

○ *TARPON TIME*

WHEN IT'S HALF-PAST May there's one place in the world I'd rather be than anywhere else—standing on the deck of a flats skiff in Everglades Bay trying to separate a tarpon from the drifting lights and shadows.

To the tarpon fisherman, Everglades Bay is home to some famous keys and banks: Rabbit, Nine Mile, Cotton, Man of War, Buchanan, and kindred others. Most of us tourists remember them as places where we lost tarpon or didn't, or saw lots of fish last time out, or didn't. The guides pay them little attention, rotating their "backcountry" fishing schedules according to the wind and tide, as well as rumor and hunch.

In the distance the mangroves seem to float on silver, and the great white wading birds stand as tall as spires. Everglades Bay is a shallow little sea, chock full of creatures making a living. The bottom is bustling with rays and bonefish grubbing in the sand. Over their heads in the deeper water, like circling fighter planes, the barracuda cruise; and over their heads, the birds circle. Now and then a splashing pelican fools me. Pointing, I ask if it is a tarpon; the guide never answers, too polite to say that by now I ought to know better.

The heavy 12-weight rod and the pound or so of reel feel good to the hand. I don't tell the guide that I've been practice-casting for a month over my half-frozen lawn. I was hoping he'd notice the difference from last year. But somehow the casts that seemed so el-

egant and long in the Northern winter have shrunk and turned gro-
tesque as I throw to imaginary fish in a hostile Southern wind. The
guide kindly says nothing as I lengthen my line, about an inch at
a time, trying to reach the backing knot or at least get close to it.
I know all too well that he can, with one or two false casts, throw
100 feet of line and make it look like you could hang clothes on it.

"Get ready," he says in a whisper. "Fish at one o'clock coming
fast."

The cast isn't perfect, but close enough so the fish sees it. I strip,
trying not to look at the fish so I won't panic and pull the fly away
too soon.

"Hit him!"

And I do, but not as hard as the guide wants.

"Hit him again!"

I offer a silent thanks that line was clear of the reel seat and my
feet as the backing melts off the reel. There's a saying that *the first
2 minutes belong to the tarpon.* I hang on and watch 6 or so feet
of silver throw itself into the air in a heart-stopping somersault 200
yards away and come down like a dropped piano. I lean into the
rod and try to slowly turn the fish. The fighting butt digs into my
belly and my arms and shoulders start to burn. I feel totally happy;
when the line goes suddenly slack I am not all that disappointed.

This time the tarpon has jumped and fallen back on the leader,
breaking it. I've lost them every way you can. The guide says,
"Let's go find you another one; I'm sure there's one out there you
can handle." I just grin up at him; we've been fishing together for
years.

"Been practicing a little?" he asks. I nod. "A little."

"Looks good," he says. High priase indeed.

"How big was the fish?" I ask.

"One-twenty, maybe one-twenty-five," he answers. I see that fish
again, turning itself over in the air, and wonder where it had been
and where it was going. How ordinary another elephant must have

seemed to Karamojo Bell ... or maybe not.

I go back to practicing my casting and finally get to where I'm working the rod, not fighting it. The casts lengthen and the guide says, "I sure wish you could throw that kind of line when there's a fish around."

"So do I," I say. "It might help if you'd learn to put the boat where the wind wasn't on my right side." He snubs the pole a little and almost pitches me off the front of the skiff.

"Talking to me?" he asks. "No," I say, "just thinking out loud."

I stare into the water until my eyes ache and play tricks, turning

Hank Brown was one of my first Islamorada tarpon guides, but he's slowly getting over the experience. He's showing me how to tie a Bimini twist—I am wondering about having a cold beer; I hate to think what Hank's wondering about, but we're still good friends.

shadows into cruising fish and seeing rolling tarpon in every other far-off ripple.

"Eleven o'clock. Single fish." I'm ready but the cast is short. I pick it up and throw again. Perfect enough! The fish is a runner; long surging pulls send a message up the line telling me about fear and the willingness to nudge death if that's the way you get to live.

I hold the rod low to the water and swing the fish up to the boat. The tarpon lies there on its side, one great eye staring past me into the sun. The guide and I look at the fish for a minute, as if it were something new that neither of us had ever seen before; then he snaps the leader, rights the fish and holds it; resting, until the gills start to work. We watch as the fish questions its freedom with little shakes of its great head. Then, gathering its majesty with a single stroke, it slides boldly away.

Ignore the passing jet ripping the afternoon apart. Forget about your debts and your trespasses. Forget the real world. Tarpon coming—a whole string of them.

○ *THE XVth DAY*

ON THE FIFTEENTH DAY, or thereabouts, God and the Recording Angel were just taking it easy. Spread out beneath them was *The Creation,* and despite last-minute changes, they were feeling rather smug with the way it had all gone; so many miracles sound easier than they really are.

God was especially interested in Adam and Eve. He considered them the centerpiece of the whole scheme, and as he watched them, he got the feeling something was a bit off.

Eve had taken to spending more and more time sitting and staring at herself in one of the pools, fussing with her hair and trying to decide which was her best side. Adam was throwing sticks in the brook and watching them sail away. As God and the Recording Angel watched, Adam threw another stick, walked over to where Eve was working on a braid, and shouted, "Back!", pointing at the stick with his finger. Eve barely gave him a glance as she stuck a large red flower in her hair, and continued to stare into the pool.

The Recording Angel finally broke the silence. "Lord," he said, "something's missing."

"I know," God said, "but I can't quite put my finger on it."

Adam was still standing close to Eve and watching another stick he'd thrown. This time they heard him say, "Back Eve!" As they watched, Eve slowly got up, waded out into the water, and brought back the stick. Just as God was about to smile, Eve swung the stick and broke it against Adam's shin.

"I think he needs a creature that will play with him," God said. He made a quick motion with his forefinger, and the stick that was lying across Adam's foot suddenly became a snake. Adam looked at it for a moment and then got another stick, waved it in front of the snake, threw it a few feet into the water, and shouted, "Back!" The snake looked at Adam in a curious way, then slithered over to where Eve sat and whispered something in her ear. Eve looked up at Adam and made a small circular motion with her finger at her temple. The snake seemed to nod in agreement, and the two of them went off together, leaving Adam standing alone by the edge of the water.

"It's not the right size or something," the Recording Angel said. "It ought to be bigger."

"I've got just the thing," God answered. The rock that Eve had been sitting on suddenly stood up and yawned, showing great shining ivory teeth. God smiled.

"What's that?" the Recording Angel asked.

"Hippo," He said, obviously pleased with himself.

Adam could see that the hippo enjoyed being in the water. He got another stick, larger than the one he'd thrown for the snake. The stick made a great splash and Adam watched expectantly as the giant beast slid into the water and disappeared. After almost an hour and no sign of the hippo, except an occasional water spout, Adam sat down on the bank and cradled his head in his arms. He was still sitting there in the fading light when Eve returned with the snake at her side. She was carrying a handful of leaves, which she tried on, looking for Adam's approval. He finally pointed at one she'd discarded and she angrily tore it in half and tossed it in the pool.

"Eve's acting a little cross, Lord," the Angel remarked.

"Well, nobody's perfect," God answered, somewhat annoyed.

It was getting dark when God turned to the Recording Angel and said, "I'm going to hold up the night for a while until we get this thing solved. What's left on inventory for delivery?"

The Recording Angel hauled out a thick scroll and began reading out loud, starting with *aardvark*. God listened attentively but did nothing more than occasionally shake his head, now and then making an outline of something in the earth with the quill-end of a long white feather. At the end of the list, the Recording Angel waited fretfully for God to ask him what a zygote was, but He didn't. The Angel was quite relieved; so much of the small stuff tended to look alike.

Suddenly God smiled. "I think I've got it," He said, waving His hand at a small passing cloud, which stopped and rained on the ground where He had been sketching. God began taking handfuls of mud and shaped them this way and that. As He worked, He spoke aloud, as if to give the Recording Angel a lesson in creating.

"It's got to be just the right size; strong, but not so big it's always knocking things over," He said. "It ought to like the water about as much as the land, so we'll give it a nice thick coat and a powerful tail—and even webbed feet!"

"You're not making another duck, are you?" the Recording Angel asked, somewhat anxiously. He knew God loved ducks, but He'd made so many already that it was difficult to tell them apart.

"No, nothing like that at all. This creature has four legs and can't fly. The really important thing is the disposition. I don't want it to ever get cross with Adam. I want it to follow him around and be good company, to please Adam more than anything else. If Adam wants to run, it will run with him; if Adam wants to play, it will play with him."

God paused for a moment and then said, "I thought Eve would be like that, but maybe I used a little too much rib."

He continued to work with the clay, broadening the head and chest, shaping the leg and tail until they were just so. He looked it over with great care, and then said in a deep and warm voice that more than hinted at His pleasure, "That's good."

The Recording Angel walked around behind him. "I really like the looks of it, Lord," he said. "What are you going to call it?"

The Lord smiled and said, "A Labrador retriever."

"Won't that be a little hard for Adam to spell?"

"No," He said, "all he has to remember is *i* before *e.*"

Then he reached out and touched the clay and said, "Sit." The glossy black hair rippled over the heavy muscles as the Labrador sat, brown eyes sparkling. He seemed to be begging to be asked to do something. God reached for the Recording Angel's staff, broke off a foot or so, and threw it. Then the Lord said, "Back!"

Instantly, the Labrador broke into a full-speed run, tumbled head-over-heels as he grabbed the stick, and brought it back. God threw it again, and the Labrador bounded off even more joyously. When he came back, God and the Recording Angel were grinning like schoolboys.

"Let me try it!" the Recording Angel asked, and threw the stick far across a distant stream. The Labrador leaped into the water, and, almost before they could believe it, was back in front of them, quivering with happiness.

The next day, the Recording Angel and God threw more sticks and the retriever, seemingly tireless, ran and swam and brought them back with an almost palpable joy. Eve stood off to one side watching them. Finally, she walked over, picked up a stick and threw it. The Labrador sat, watching. When she cried, "Back," he leaped into the air and almost flew into the water. Eve laughed as the droplets wet her. When he returned and gave her the stick, she took it and playfully tugged his ear. The Labrador raised his head and licked her hand. God and the Recording Angel watched her smile; it was radiant in its loveliness.

"I think I'll make one for Eve," God said.

"Exactly the same?" asked the Recording Angel.

"Yes and no," God replied.

The Recording Angel had made his staff whole again and stood leaning on it for the longest while. Then in a very quiet voice, he said, "Lord, would it be too much to ask you to make one more? Then we could keep it here just to make sure it's perfect."

The Lord smiled and said, "I was thinking the very same thing."

Book Design by Karen Massad

Printed and Bound by Arcata Graphics/Fairfield